T0055553

The Art of SERIES

EDITED BY CHARLES BAXTER

The Art of series is a line of books reinvigorating the practice of craft and criticism. Each book is a brief, witty, and useful exploration of fiction, nonfiction, or poetry by a writer impassioned by a singular craft issue. *The Art of* volumes provide a series of sustained examinations of key, but sometimes neglected, aspects of creative writing by some of contemporary literature's finest practitioners.

The Art of Description: World into Word by Mark Doty

The Art of the Poetic Line by James Longenbach

The Art of Daring: Risk, Restlessness, Imagination
by Carl Phillips

The Art of Attention: A Poet's Eye by Donald Revell

The Art of Time in Fiction: As Long As It Takes
by Joan Silber

The Art of Syntax: Rhythm of Thought, Rhythm of Song
by Ellen Bryant Voigt

*The Art of Recklessness: Poetry as Assertive Force and
Contradiction* by Dean Young

THE ART OF DARING

RISK, RESTLESSNESS, IMAGINATION

Also by Carl Phillips

POETRY

Silverchest
Double Shadow
Speak Low
Quiver of Arrows: Selected Poems, 1986–2006
Riding Westward
The Rest of Love
Rock Harbor
The Tether
Pastoral
From the Devotions
Cortège
In the Blood

PROSE

*Coin of the Realm: Essays on the Life and
    Art of Poetry*

TRANSLATION

Philoctetes by Sophocles

The Art of

DARING

RISK, RESTLESSNESS, IMAGINATION

Carl Phillips

Graywolf Press

This publication is made possible, in part, by the voters of Minnesota through a Minnesota State Arts Board Operating Support grant, thanks to a legislative appropriation from the arts and cultural heritage fund, and through grants from the National Endowment for the Arts and the Wells Fargo Foundation Minnesota. Significant support has also been provided by Target, the McKnight Foundation, Amazon.com, and other generous contributions from foundations, corporations, and individuals. To these organizations and individuals we offer our heartfelt thanks.

Published by Graywolf Press
250 Third Avenue North, Suite 600
Minneapolis, Minnesota 55401

www.graywolfpress.org

Published in the United States of America

ISBN 978-1-55597-681-1

    4   6   8   9   7   5   3

Library of Congress Control Number: 2013958014

Cover design: Scott Sorenson

Outdoors the leaves was rustling, different
from when I'd went in. It was coming on a rain.
The day had a two-way look, like a day will at
change of the year—clouds dark and the gold air
still in the road . . .

—Eudora Welty, *The Golden Apples*

Contents

Preface

In a matter of days, the backyard has filled with leaves—catalpa, pear, chestnut, tower of pin oak, twist of dogwood: When did it become fall again? How did I get here? What is this place?

Life and art are of course different from each other, but their unavoidable relationship—like that of a coin's two sides sometimes, and other times like that between an image and the mirror's return of it—means that art and life are forever *part* of the same thing. Hard to say what that thing is, exactly, not coin, not mirror.

I think restlessness—of imagination, but also bodily, by which I have mostly meant sexual, I see that now—is what brings us to that space where art and life not only *seem* interchangeable, for a moment they *are* so, space where they penetrate one another, space in which, caught between the two, we can be variously lost, broken, or we can summon that daring that can bring us—loss and brokenness in tow—to unknowing. When I speak of unknowing, I don't mean ignorance so much as a kind of removal of all the trappings of presentation—how we present ourselves to the world—and an accompanying exposure of the usually hidden parts, what we hide equally from others and from ourselves.

Foliage hides the tree that we know in winter. Both trees are the same tree, aren't they, the one sporting leaves, the one laid bare? Is what hides us any less valid than what's hidden? Is it any less difficult to look squarely upon our secrets than upon the ways in which we fashion a self for presentation—literature of course being one of those ways; literature as, also, the presentation itself . . .

This book began as the three essays with which it opens. I'd been asked to speak on art, and I figured the craft of poetry seemed appropriate: I'd corral a handful of poems, discuss how they work and the ways in which how they work might contribute to how and what they mean. Soon enough, though, I realized how the poems shared restlessness as a subject (and often a method); more to the point, though, these were the poems that had attracted me—which said what, about me?

"As if distortion were preferable to reality. Isn't it sometimes?" Do I still think that? I believe reality can become distorted past recognition, and it's in these moments that only something like daring, a willingness to risk going forward when we hardly know where we are, can provide us the chance both for self-knowledge and for the making of art. Restlessness carries us to penetration—we pierce the world as we knew it, the world as we've never known it pierces us, in turn, daring pushes us past this . . . and then what?

Who can say which is better, the glory of foliage or the truth of what's left when the leaves fall away?

For the artist, life is more than a journey we're on, it's an active questing—it requires stamina, risk, a sense of daring in the face of risk, the risk being many things: we may have dared for nothing, we may have lost more than we expected to, or we may triumph—that is, arrive at the art to which restlessness (ambition in its natural state), with luck, can toss us, but at a cost, one that can take years to be understood.

> not what manner of end they came to—
> that part is legend—but to what degree, having found
> you must, you must call it something, you will call it
>
> inevitable. Deserved, even. Maybe worth what it cost.

So ends my earlier book of essays, *Coin of the Realm.* Ten years ago. This book is much less of a book on craft than that one was. It serves, I hope, as more a meditation on what it can mean to live a life through art, to make art from a life, or parts of it, and—when art and life seem impossibly blurred—to insist on a difference between living a life and doing more than that, instead choosing to dare a life.

THE ART OF DARING

RISK, RESTLESSNESS,
IMAGINATION

Restlessness

Little Gods of Making

A friend tells me we are, all of us, little gods of making, here on earth to make some part of us we can leave behind, a way of translating *making* into *made—made* as a kind of death, or closure, to the act of *making*. It's as if the trajectory of art were necessarily that of life itself, with art having perhaps more resonance than the body-in-death. Or perhaps it's more accurate to say there's a different resonance, since the body-in-death has its own haunting, unforgettable, and often unbearable qualities, from which we walk away at last not unchanged.

"It's a human need, to give to shapelessness a form." So I said once, in an earlier poem, referring specifically to the human impulse to make something concrete out of an abstraction like love—hence, relationships, the various configurations of making a life with someone else. But while it may be true that humans deal with the particular shapelessness of abstractions, the impulse to give or make form is evident throughout the natural world. Out of the general shapelessness of straw and thread, for example, birds fashion a nest, the form of the nest designed to accommodate the bird's body and the bodies that will also live there later. Animals tend toward social forms—coyotes into packs, fish into schools, making out of the directionless (because unassigned) individual body a community of bodies, each given a place in the social order, all for the purpose of survival—which is to say that the motivation, instinctively, is to again accommodate the body, by protecting it. Form, shape—these may be our only way, finally, of making sense of the world around us. And the body may be the one form, finally, from which we begin, each time, our knowing. This makes sense, given that we are born into form—each of us *is* a former shapelessness that acquired physical form, and the general impulse is to create forms that will accommodate the protection of that *ur*-form, as it were, the body.

Houses, societies—these accommodate the physical protection of the body. Art, I would like to suggest, accommodates the psychic/psychological protection of the body—something required specifically by humans (as opposed to coyotes, birds, fish) because of that self-consciousness that is unique to human beings, our ability to be *aware* of such things as mortality, and to think in terms of ethics and of moral valence . . .

There's a yard that I've walked my dog past for years—we'd stop each day and wait for the dog tied up there to notice us, come toward us, and then do the brief sniff-and-greet that dogs do. That dog died last winter, but all this past summer, whenever we walked past that yard, my dog would stop, look into the empty yard, wag her tail—then we'd move on. This may be memory, on my dog's part, but not recognition exactly, and certainly not grief. Nor does passing the yard conjure in the dog any loose meditation on loss, animal awareness of it, or of regret. That's the beauty of being an animal, and the sometime curse of being a human being. It's a curse, though, that is catalyst, too, for the making of art.

Here is a poem by Louise Bogan, called "Night":

The cold remote islands
And the blue estuaries
Where what breathes, breathes
The restless wind of the inlets,
And what drinks, drinks
The incoming tide;

Where shell and weed
Wait upon the salt wash of the sea,
And the clear nights of stars
Swing their lights westward
To set behind the land;

Where the pulse clinging to the rocks
Renews itself forever;
Where, again on cloudless nights,
The water reflects
The firmament's partial setting;

—O remember
In your narrowing dark hours
That more things move
Than blood in the heart.

What I've always admired most immediately in this poem is its camera work, the way in which the reader's eye is so carefully controlled. In stanza one, it's as if we're looking straight out, into a remoteness whose inhabitants are unspecifiable, "what breathes," "what drinks." With stanza two, we get the specifics of shell and weed, assignable to the shore, and the stars, assignable to sky; which is to say, we have moved from looking out, and are now directed downward to the shore and sea, then upward to the night sky, and then—by the anticipation of the stars' setting—back to the land they will set behind. The same movements occur in stanza three—downward to the rocks, upward to the sky (implied by "cloudless"), downward to the water, then upward, via reflection, to the firmament (and again, the mention of "setting," to imply the horizon of land). In the course of three stanzas, we look into a generality of world, only to learn that what appears general has its specific zones of earth, sea, and sky, which—when we look more repeatedly (are *made* to do so, in stanza three)—seem the fixed and timeless points around and within which all else "merely" occurs, then ceases to do so. This recognition is the trigger for the camera's final move—the camera, which has looked out into the physical, natural world, swings to an interior that is human, *meta*physical, self-reflective, and too often forgetful of and/or resistant to the self's relative irrelevance within the world it inhabits and the limitedness of the self's existence, as we see the ongoing, cyclical interaction of the sea, earth, and sky juxtaposed with the "narrowing dark hours" that characterize human life.

Camera work is one level at which Bogan's poem can be seen as an enactment of the mind passing from mere observation to a kind of curiosity that in turn leads to closer observation, which then leads to understanding. What gets understood is sobering. Also disturbing. Also strangely comforting: to understand one's transience in the world—one's irrelevance *to* it—can be a way to begin assigning less weight to our various crises, whether those of triumph or defeat; and from here, the diminishment both of arrogance and of self-pity becomes possible.

This doesn't change how disturbing it also is, to recognize that we will die, while the world will continue,
utterly indifferent to our having existed. The difficulty of
reaching this understanding gets enacted in the syntax
of Bogan's poem. To begin with, the first three stanzas
are all part of what turns out to be a single, incomplete
sentence. We're led to *believe* there will be resolution;
subordinate clauses create anticipation—we anticipate a
governing sentence within which these clauses have
been embedded. We get a total of five clauses that hinge
on the word *where* in the first three stanzas:

> where A breathes
> where B drinks
>
> where shell and weed wait
> and the clear nights of stars swing
>
> where the pulse renews itself
> where the water reflects

These presumably occur within a main sentence, yes?
The subject of the sentence is announced from the start:
"The cold remote islands / And the blue estuaries"—
what about them? we might ask—which is to say, we
want a verb, to tell us something about their existence
or their activity. Instead, we keep coming up against

clauses that stall the arrival of a verb by continuing to refocus on what occurs within the space defined by islands and estuaries and then by the earth and sky. The relative clauses are where physical vision gets refined to the point of clarity that leads to metaphysical understanding. The clauses can also be seen as a stubbornness, at the level of syntax—the mind balks, falters, as it approaches a difficult truth—the sentence refuses to conclude, except via the nonconclusion of a semicolon at the end of the third stanza; the main verb never gets delivered. It's as if the mind were saying "I can't," "I won't," and then "I must"—and with that, the poem leaps into recognition. That leap gets signaled by the abandoning of a long fragment for a briefer, complete sentence, the abandoning of the declarative voice for the imperative—the command to "remember"—and the abandoning of the exterior world of geography for the interior of the self, the human "you" that had been nowhere apparent in the poem before.

All poems contain tension of one kind or another. Or, to be specific, any poem that has resonance will contain tension. One tension in Bogan's poem is between the stalling I've described already and the relentlessness with which the poem's form marches steadily forward. The syntax stalls, but the stanza length, moving from a six-line stanza, to two five-line stanzas, to a final stanza of four lines, diminishes, reflective of the poem's argument that the world is larger than the self, the self that accordingly receives the fewest lines.

That is one level of tension. But another occurs between the self receiving only four lines and the fact that those lines are the poem's final stanza—arguably a poem's most important stanza. Which is it? Are we irrelevant? Or are we everything that at last the world comes down to? I would say this is the main tension of Bogan's poem. And the fact that both things are true gives the poem its resonance: we can understand our relative unimportance within the grand scheme of life, but we are incapable of seeing the world through any other lens before seeing it first through the lens of our individual selves. My world is not my dog's world, and yet the world itself is the same world. Bogan's poem exhorts us to try remembering that human existence and endeavor are not the only things—are perhaps the least things. But we are human, and to us, they are everything.

$$\equiv$$

The predicted tropical storm arrived late this morning, and by late afternoon was at hurricane pitch. And in ac-cordance with what by now is pretty much ritual, my partner and I drove up the coast, to see the storm's full impact. Parked up at Nauset Heights, at a landing that no one else has managed to find, we've got an uninterrupted view of the ocean—powerful, violent. There's a cracked dinghy that someone forgot to bring in; the wind must have taken it and smashed it against the rock it now rests beside. There's a section of wooden fencing that has come apart, after the dune that it held gave way—again, the wind, the water.

Turning to Doug, I say, "I think what attracts me to storms is the way they reduce form to formlessness. Or no, that's not it. A storm revises a thing's original form. It isn't formlessness, it's revision."

To all of which, Doug answers by saying, "There's nothing better than a great storm." He's a photographer, a landscape photographer, the kind whose instinct is to see the world first for what it is, not for what it may conjure up in the mind. Clarity of vision, not distortion of it. This is not to say that he isn't capable of seeing the various other resonances of a landscape, but that comes later, I think. I'm the kind of poet who thinks in the opposite manner, tending to see first what a thing resembles, and only afterward—almost reluctantly—do I see it for what it actually is. As if distortion were preferable to reality. Isn't it, sometimes? Isn't this what Bogan's poem is also saying?

Meanwhile, to see a thing only for what it physically is, is its own distortion. For human beings, the world is not experienced purely through the senses, but through consciousness, histories private and public, individual notions of right and wrong, and an inability to resist entirely an urge to anthropomorphize. The term for a tree whose limbs grow downward, instead of up and out, is *weeping*. As if it were sad. As if a tree could *be* sad.

=

It would be freeing, indeed, to inhabit a world stripped of resonance—for a time at least. "No ideas but in things," says William Carlos Williams. Things are what they are—that may be so; but why do they so swiftly have nuances, connotations? Why, for some of us, do they almost always? These are among the questions behind James Schuyler's poem "Procession," a poem whose form enacts the struggle between an impulse toward resonance and a longing for it to spare us, just a little:

> Serene and purple twilight of the South
> the wind-distorted olives
> so dim beside the road
> so very still tonight
> the sea delicately touches
> the shore with foam
>
> Black clad, glimmer of white
> pyramids of trembling gold

> up the white road wind
> in misty iris blue
>
> a cross, a crown, a spear
>
> the air is drenched
>
> the nails, the hammer
>
> fragrance of lemon and orange
>
> the scourge, a sponge
>
> salt perfume of the sea

The juxtaposition is set up in the first two stanzas. The first stanza presents us with the natural world—serene, purple, a delicacy to the sea's touches; though we could also say the eye here is a bit idealistic—the sea isn't always delicate, of course; and there's a hint of an impulse to cast what is less than ideal into the background, as we note how the twilight has put a dimness upon distortion in that phrase "the wind-distorted olives / so dim beside the road" (lines 2–3).

But immediately following this stanza is the religious procession, the participants clad in black and white, and bearing torches or candles—so I am reading the image "pyramids of trembling gold" (8). With that juxtaposition, the natural world, free of connotation, gets pitched against nothing less than the crucifixion that marks that zone in Christianity between Old Testament vengeance and New Testament mercy and salvation. The poem's observer cannot see a religious procession without the procession suggesting something of the history of the faith behind that procession, hence the immediate images that spring to mind: "a cross, a crown, a spear" (11). From that line to the poem's end, there's a patterned monostichic shuttling between crucifixion imagery and images that spring purely from the natural world—the air, the scent of citrus on it, the smell of the sea. As if the speaker were hoping to push away the image of suffering by focusing instead on the natural world? Is the tone of the last six lines that of insistence?

Another way to read those last six lines is as coming all from the same scene. Perhaps the speaker, in remembering the crucifixion, now fleshes out, as it were, the remembered scene—imagining that, at the time of the crucifixion, the air might well have been drenched, have smelled of citrus and the sea. If this is the case, then another way to read these last lines is as an implied assertion about suffering: that, while suffering takes place, the world continues—as indeed it does. It continues and does so fairly oblivious to our human endeavors, the same realization that Bogan arrived at in her poem. And this realization might understandably trigger a response whereby we want to push away human reality for an idealized natural world—which takes us back to our first way of reading the poem's last six lines, namely, as an enactment of the mind refusing the imagery of suffering. Note, too, that the imagery of suffering is also synonymous with the human-made— cross, crown, spear, nails, hammer, scourge, sponge: all human-made, concrete, versus the abstract, sensual world of drenchedness, fragrance, perfume, all of it attachable to the natural elements of, respectively, air, lemon and orange, and the sea. So there's another level of tension, not just between suffering and natural beauty, but also between the human-made and the natural.

Can all of these things be at work in the poem? Is there a need to choose?

There may not be a need to choose, but there is usually, eventually, a desire for closure, for some choice to be made. Schuyler gives an even number of lines to the suffering and to what I'll call beauty. They are exactly in balance, we might say. But beauty is the note on which the poem ends, so that, for a moment, it can feel as if beauty is the victor, has in a sense put a halt to the debate by resolving it. That sense of closure occurs at the level of sound, as well—if we read the poem aloud, eventually the words end and we stop speaking. But look at how the first two stanzas opened with a capital letter—announcing a new stanza and, at first thought, a sentence; in both these stanzas, however, we've been misled: Each stanza is a fragment. Each began, orthographically, as a sentence, but no verb appears, hence the stanzas do not end with a period (I note that stanza one does *contain* a complete sentence—"the sea delicately touches / the shore with foam"—but it appears embedded *within* the fragment, thanks to there being no capital letters to show where a sentence might begin). After these two stanzas, we have the six monostichs, nowhere capitalized, and yet clearly not part of an earlier sentence; instead, the elements float, list-like, processionally, and the absence of a period at the poem's end implies that there is no end—the words have ended, but without conclusion. Note too that in the three places where there is punctuation—the commas that occur in the stanzas containing the tools of crucifixion—the effect is to generate a list within a single line, an ongoing series that ends by not ending, in unpunctuated white space.

So there's an ongoingness conveyed by the relative lack both of punctuation and of capitalization, but at the level of sound there's a sense of conclusion. And in the tension between these two lies the resonance without which a poem is flat, static, which is to say, is not a poem. This resonance can be frustrating for the reader who wants experience to be translated; but poems tend instead to transform, not translate—they are indeed translations of felt and thought experience into verbal presentation, but their business, as it were, is to transform experience so that our assumption about a given experience can be disturbed and, accordingly, our thinking *about* that experience might be at once made more complicated, deeper, richer. This doesn't mean that we as readers necessarily will *feel* better. But the purpose of reading poetry is not, to my mind, to be made to feel better, but rather to understand human experience more entirely; this kind of understanding leads to wisdom, not the good feeling that is finally a shallow version of the happiness that wisdom strangely brings in its wake.

Closure is more comforting than self-abandon, in the long run. It feels good to lie in the middle of a field in the pitch dark, until it doesn't and we begin to wonder who or what might be out there that we cannot see. Hence, the comfort of a room or at least of bearings. Even animals have a tendency to sleep with something behind them—a wall, a tree, a hillside—so that one side, at least, can be protected. This is equivalent, I would argue, to the comforts of rhyme and rhythm in a poem—there's an ease and pleasure to memorizing, say, a sonnet by Shakespeare, once we know that the rhymes will occur in predictable places, the lines will have a predictable number of stresses, and there will be a consistent *number* of lines, namely, fourteen.

But this comfort will not lead to resonance, if the argument of a poem is as regular as the poem's form, or if there aren't other points of tension—between, say, the regularity of rhyme and the irregularity of sentence length, or between sentence length and line length. Look at how that works in Shakespeare's Sonnet 129:

Th'expense of spirit in a waste of shame
Is lust in action; and till action, lust
Is perjured, murd'rous, bloody, full of blame,
Savage, extreme, rude, cruel, not to trust;
Enjoyed no sooner but despised straight;
Past reason hunted, and no sooner had,
Past reason hated as a swallowed bait,
On purpose laid to make the taker mad;
Mad in pursuit, and in possession so,
Had, having, and in quest to have, extreme;
A bliss in proof, and proved, a very woe;
Before, a joy proposed; behind, a dream.
       All this the world well knows, yet none knows
          well
       To shun the heaven that leads men to this hell.

As you can see, there's the expected scheme (formal) of a Shakespearean sonnet: an alternation of rhymes within each four-line segment, and then two lines that rhyme right next to each other. At the level of sound, this means that we are wobbling, as it were, between rhymes—that is, the rhymes are interrupted—before settling on the two rhyming lines no longer separated from each other. Which is to say, the feeling is that of arrival, of closure, sonically speaking. But—also characteristic of a Shakespearean sonnet—the rhyming two lines of conclusion often—as here—tend to sum up, or offer an Aesop-like moral via which to understand what's been said earlier: "All this the world well knows, yet none knows well / To shun the heaven that leads men to this hell." It *sounds* like resolve, yes, but what the lines actually *say* is that no one has figured out how to deal with the corrosive realities of lust, which have been disturbingly outlined in lines 1–12. So there's a meaningful tension here between formal and sonic regularity and the irresolvability of the poem's argument—there is no solution, that is, to lust, not even the hoped-for solution of knowledge-via-experience; there is only the temporary stay that the sonnet's form gives to human predicament.

I mentioned sentence length earlier. It's intriguing to realize this is a sonnet composed of a mere two sentences. One—the one devoted to detailing the effects of lust—happens to be twelve lines long; the other, the one where knowledge or wisdom comes to the fore, is a couplet. This is another level on which the poem enacts its argument. At the level of sentence length, lust outweighs reason, twelve to two, or by 600 percent. In addition, this sentence-level irregularity is in tension with the regularity of form everywhere else in the sonnet—what appears to be regular both is and isn't, and this contributes to the poem's resonance, which again comes not from closure but from *apparent* closure of a poem's argument. We long for closure, for completeness. As the poet Lyn Hejinian puts it in her poem "Slowly":

> Of course completeness has a strong appeal
>   It can provide emotional satisfaction and even,
> as in the case of a job well done, material satisfaction,
> it can be exhilarating to finish a work of art, it can be
> a relief, having cleaned up after a dull and awkward
> party, to stand in the relative silence of one's restored
> idiosyncratic order and say "That's over!"—these are
> not words of regret

But some part of a good reader of poetry understands that closure, for human beings, is a construct, not a reality, and the resonance that might frustrate some is ultimately more authoritative because more expressive of

what it means to be human, for better *and* for worse.
Here's Hejinian again:

> . . .[D]efiance of closure is what constitutes
>   adventurousness patiently
> We're at will
> We're with world (return)
> Remains of the present remaining in view remain this
>   *and* that.

=

It's often assumed that a resistance to closure is a post-
modern development, but I hope I'm making clear
that *any* successful poem—one that is true to human
experience—will resist closure. To be resonant *is* to resist absolute closure. Homer's *Iliad* may end with the
death of the hero Hector and the eventual ransoming
of and funeral rites for his body, but that is only the
end of the narrative, not a final statement about death,
heroism, or grief—there *is* no final statement to be
made about these subjects; rather, the *Iliad* leaves us to
meditate, in the wake of its narrative, on its more metaphysical questions, even if they are only implied: Who
are we? What is ambition? What is death and its relationship to memory? To what degree is great achievement in a life a guarantee of our being remembered,

and what difference can it possibly make, if we're dead already?

＝

There are as many reasons to make a poem as there are to read one, surely. I've been thinking it might be like amateur photography—how the main reason to take so many pictures of fairly ordinary—or even extraordinary—situations is to say "we were here, this happened." And perhaps, too, a kind of stay against forgetting, against *being* forgotten, not just by those who may come after us, but by our later selves. "I was that person, I remember, he seems all but a stranger to me now . . ." Are we not somehow back to that very old question of "who am I?"

Another reason for making—and this is certainly my own reason for doing so—is as a way of understanding not entirely but a bit more clearly what resists solution. I think it's important for the maker—the poet, to stay with what I know best—to understand from the start that solution is impossible, even as he or she nevertheless attempts it. A careful calibration of humility and arrogance is required, with maybe a healthy dose of foolhardiness and/or masochism, take your pick, thrown in. Or to speak from personal experience, I tend to begin writing a poem with a sense that

I know how to navigate the territory I'm entering—it's not until the end, or more likely halfway through, that I remember the truth, abandon myself again to being lost, and just hope to arrive somewhere wiser, though no less lost, in one piece.

The thing that gives me that initial, misleading confidence about my psychological bearings is the set of bearings I establish at the level of structure. I think every poet does this, each one differently. In Shakespeare's Sonnet 129, the structure was a fairly regular one, at first glance. But even a poem with no formal regularity has a form: a certain number of lines, for example—that's enough to say a poem has a form. W. S. Merwin's poem "Elegy" reads thus, in its unpunctuated entirety:

Who would I show it to

In terms of form, we can say this is a one-line poem of six words, the sentence itself cast in the interrogative, as a question that arises in response to the title: who would I show an *elegy* to is presumably what is meant, the implication being that there is no one, the speaker is that alone, abandoned, isolated—is that not an elegy?

Somewhere between the more or less fixed structure of the Shakespearean sonnet and the monostich exemplified by Merwin's "Elegy" can be found the blues stanza, or what I think I'll call the blues strophe, since it isn't always contained within a single stanza. The blues strophe consists of three movements (not necessarily three lines, but often three sentences), in the course of which an idea is put forth, pushed a tad further, and then pushed to what feels comparatively like resolution. (One could, in fact, argue that the psychological and rhetorical structure of the blues stanza are not all that different from what happens in the course of the first three quatrains of a sonnet by Shakespeare, especially in the earlier sonnets.) Two fairly representative blues strophes are this one from W. C. Handy's "St. Louis Blues":

> Gypsy done tole me, "Don't you wear no black."
> Yes she done tole me, "Don't you wear no black,
> Go to St. Louis. You can win him back."

and this, from Langston Hughes's "Morning After":

> I was so sick last night I
> Didn't hardly know my mind.
> So sick last night I
> Didn't know my mind.
> I drunk some bad licker that
> Almost made me blind.

The effect of a blues strophe is to at once push something a little further away and, by staying with it—

revising it—to bring it a little more closely into focus; often enough, sorrow is pushed further away by being brought into a perspective that allows the speaker to remember that sorrow can only exist in the context of joy and laughter. The blues in this regard has always seemed to me one of the most human forms of expression, because it is fluid and also because it is resonant with the multifacetedness of human experience.

Gayl Jones uses a loose version of a blues strophe to structure her poem "Deep Song":

The blues calling my name.
She is singing a deep song.
She is singing a deep song.
I am human.
He calls me crazy.
He says, "You must be
crazy."
I say, "Yes, I'm crazy."
He sits with his knees apart.
His fly is broken.
She is singing a deep song.
He smiles.
She is singing a deep song.
"Yes, I'm crazy."
I care about you.
I care.

I care about you.
I care.
He lifts his eyebrows.
The blues is calling my name.
I tell him he'd better
do something about his fly.
He says something softly.
He says something so softly
that I can't even hear him.
He is a dark man.
Sometimes he is a good dark man.
Sometimes he is a bad dark man.
I love him.

What a strange poem. Part of the strangeness has to do, I think, with a psychological claustrophobia. Very little is happening, except in the Henry James sense of things happening: gestures, statements that mean more, presumably, than what they say—"You must be crazy"; "Yes, I'm crazy." And rising more clearly as the poem proceeds, a sense that this relationship is decidedly one-sided: she cares about *him;* she loves *him*—whether or not her feelings are matched by his isn't said; but the clues—his broken fly, his knees spread apart, the lifted eyebrows, the fact that he can be in equal parts a good and a bad man—these suggest a relationship where the speaker loves him against her own better thinking. Maybe this is what she means by "I am human." Namely, she knows how she *should* feel, and she knows how she *feels,* and the two are very different indeed, and coexistent, even as the man coexists both as good and as bad. They are *both* human.

Is this a love poem?

Is this a poem of sorrow?

A poem about our sometimes inability to help ourselves, no matter how clear we are as to why we need help?

Yes. Yes. And yes. Which is to say, the poem is a resonant one, authoritative because it resists easy solution—at the level of form, Jones does this by having the blues strophe routinely disrupt its own progress, starting with the first three lines, which I consider an aborted blues strophe. You can see how the second line is a pushing forward of the first line—the blues calling my name; well, actually, she's singing my name, the deep song of it. But with line 3, we get a kind of stutter, not progress, just repetition. And the subject shifts abruptly at line 4.

The next blues strophe can be found in lines 5–8: again, some forward motion, from the statement that he calls her crazy, to our actually hearing him say it. But her answer merely agrees with his statement, instead of revising it—a complete blues strophe would more likely go thus:

> He calls me crazy.
> He says, "You must be
> crazy."
> I say, "Yes, I'm crazy,
> but so are you."

So again, an interruption of progress. We'll see a similar situation in the repetition at lines 15–18 ("I care about you. / I care. / I care about you. / I care"), lines that also repeat themselves in their lineation. At lines 23–25, we are again in the zone of the blues, the one statement getting pushed further, revised—"He says something softly. / He says something so softly / that I can't even hear him"—and there is resolution, of a sort, in "that I can't even hear him," except that we're no closer to what it is he says.

What's been happening, then, is that the blues strophe or would-be blues strophe keeps appearing, and then failing to resolve. Parallel, I would argue, with the sensibility behind the speaker herself, coming closer to clarity, then in a sense refusing it. Lines 26–28 make up the final blues strophe to be found within this one-stanzaed poem—but again, none of the forward thrust that should occur:

> He is a dark man.
> Sometimes he is a good dark man.
> Sometimes he is a bad dark man.

There is revision from being a dark man to a good dark man. But the fact that he is also a bad dark man doesn't so much *revise* the previous statement about goodness as add another element that neither negates nor corroborates the previous statement. Both the good and the bad of the man are true. Part of the force of the poem's conclusion—"I love him"—comes from the confidence with which it either refuses or embraces the man's two-sidedness. It's hard to say for sure. It's an expression of feeling, not of reason, it's a pitching of absoluteness in the face of ambivalence, it's an expression of calculated risk and of recklessness, both. And it makes the speaker sad, noble, and exactly what she says she is: human.

I think it's largely the conundrum of being human that makes us keep making. I think it has something to do with revision—how, not only is the world in constant revision, but each of us is, as well. Each new experience at some level becomes a part of that lens through which we see—as in understand—the world we pass through. Yes, the solutions continue to elude us, but we ourselves are also in motion—or to put it another way, as we try to solve for the x of ourselves, we find we are not the selves today that we were just yesterday. Which means the world as we know it has shifted somewhat. We begin our quest again. The hand finds the pen, and the pen the page. And, very slowly, what was silent begins opening.

On Restlessness

And I saw that restlessness was neither the problem, nor the solution. Was just the fact. A force. And though eventually it might break me, I would not refuse it.

It is probably human to prefer certainty to uncertainty. The idea would seem to be that uncertainty is a form of instability, and instability is difficult to associate with the usual notions of happiness, or of living "the good life," namely, a life as free of anxiety as possible, and what does uncertainty bring with it, if not anxiety, against which we're increasingly told we should medicate ourselves: take this, you'll feel at ease in a crowd of people, you'll sleep at night, you won't feel sad. It's this resistance to uncertainty that lies behind a general preference for accessibility in our society—in music, film, literature, yes, but also in such things as food, the colors to paint a house's interior. Accessibility means that a thing should be immediately available to us via the *usual* means. This can only come about if the means of access to a thing remains fixed. Most people don't want to go to a movie that they don't "get" at the end, one that challenges their fixed notions about what life is, what a movie is. Uncertainty disturbs, it challenges us where we had felt comfortable, it unsettles us. But without it, we merely get older, we never deepen.

=

What is the relationship between restlessness and uncertainty? Clearly uncertainty can be a *catalyst* for restlessness—in our not being able to know something absolutely, we somewhere have to acknowledge a vulnerability in ourselves. In knowledge is safety, of at least a sort; what we don't know might not hurt us, but it *could,* insofar as we can't rule out entirely that it *can't.* The general consensus is likely to be for avoiding harm as well as those places where harm is possible.

But there is a sensibility that—instinctively, most likely unconsciously—recognizes vulnerability as a space of possible nourishment. For such a sensibility, the impulse is not to shun the unknown, but to offer the self up to it, for the chance to know the self more fully than before: for at least one way in which we come to know ourselves comes from observing how we weather or do not weather any given challenge. Besides getting to know the self better, we get to know, or get a sense of knowing, the unknown to which we've committed ourselves—at the very least, we gain a knowledge of what an engaged relationship between the self and the unknowable can mean. For the religious, the translation for that engaged relationship is faith, and the unknowable is deity of one sort or another. I'm thinking of faith here as a kind of crucible in which the believer comes perhaps not to know entirely but to deepen an existing understanding of—and in turn, faith in—divinity. For the artist, the poet specifically, the poem is both the translation for that engaged relationship between self and unknown, and it is the record of it. As for the unknown/unknowable, I think it's all those *other* selves within us that are both part of and separate from our conscious selves—memory, dream, demons perhaps better left undisturbed, perhaps not. A poet writes about any number of things, but whether confessional or not, every poem is in part a record of an engagement between our conscious and unconscious selves—it is why the writing of poetry can be so dangerous. We are likely to learn more than we planned on, in the course of making. We thought we knew a thing. Now we know it differently. That's the effect of the poem on its maker and it should also, ideally, be the effect for the reader of the poem.

Poetry—the kind that does in fact give us the world as we had not seen it, that makes us question what we had thought we knew (and this is finally the only thing I am willing to *call* poetry)—poetry is the result of a generative restlessness of imagination. Such an imagination experiences uncertainty not as adversary but as opportunity, not as an object of fear but, for better or worse, an object of an all-but-impossible-to-resist fascination. These uncertainties become the obsessions to be wrestled with, as it were—and with luck, the result is poetry: the poem as, again, evidence and record of the mind's approach to, grappling with, and (if only temporarily) having mastered an uncertainty by putting it in a place, a context, for greater understanding. The poems that most persuade me of their authority are those that leave room for further uncertainty once they're over. The *illusion* is one of mastery, but somewhere the creative mind recognizes, with time, that absolute mastery of an idea has proved again elusive, we approach the old uncertainty from a new angle, it continues to fascinate by its very resistance to us, and we are on our way to the next poem.

=

Of course, there are poems that "merely," we might say, record that something happened, a feeling was felt; or perhaps they play with structure, sound, and rhythm "merely" because it is possible to do so. Robert Adams, in his book *Beauty in Photography*, puts it this way—speaking of painting, but it applies as well to poetry:

> Some of what in our time we have called art has been concerned solely and finally, I believe, with perceptual form, that is, form completely free of any conceptual content, form purely of ordered sensation; the pleasures we associate with it are exclusively those of color and shape and texture. Setting aside the artists' intent, works by Josef Albers, Jackson Pollock, and Frank Stella are conspicuous examples. Insofar as art has occupied itself in this fashion, it seems to offer real but minor pleasures, the joys of decoration.

I am instead speaking here of the poems that tend to last over time—those that, whether directly or indirectly, concern themselves finally with the large abstractions that resist solution: love, death, grief, joy, aggression, desire: words—subjects, even—often deemed inappropriate for contemporary poetry. And yet, what distinguishes being human if not self-consciousness, which in turn allows us to understand and conceive of abstraction in the first place? Since when was poetry not *about* and *of* human feeling? I write poetry for the same reason that I read it, both as a way of being alive and as a way of trying to understand what it means—how it feels—to be alive.

=

Another way to think of restlessness: as a form of ambition. Unsatisfied with the given—the usual explanations, the usual goals for and trappings of a life—there are those who push past the given, are willing to enter into uncertainty—to take a risk—in order to get to something presumably superior and/or preferable to "the old life." I don't mean corporate ambitions, the kind that can lead to an increase of money and power and material possessions—I mean the quest for meaning, for heightened feeling, for expanded vision, even if that should mean that we arrive at what disturbs, leaving us more unsettled, less at rest than we had been. This, I would argue, is the artist's sensibility. And I'll point out that it's not a perverse desire for being disturbed; it's instead both a recognition that growth can't happen without disturbance, and a realistic understanding of the world as a place where pleasure and its opposite coexist—the artist refuses to ignore it, or perhaps more accurately the artist is incapable of ignoring it, because of a commitment to a knowledge that is absolute, entire, and at last elusive.

That doesn't mean, though, that we can't regret the knowledge that we come into. One is human, after all.

=

Here is Frost's "After Apple-Picking":

My long two-pointed ladder's sticking through a tree
Toward heaven still,
And there's a barrel that I didn't fill
Beside it, and there may be two or three
Apples I didn't pick upon some bough.
But I am done with apple-picking now.
Essence of winter sleep is on the night,
The scent of apples: I am drowsing off.
I cannot rub the strangeness from my sight
I got from looking through a pane of glass
I skimmed this morning from the drinking trough
And held against the world of hoary grass.
It melted, and I let it fall and break.
But I was well
Upon my way to sleep before it fell,
And I could tell
What form my dreaming was about to take.
Magnified apples appear and disappear,
Stem end and blossom end,

And every fleck of russet showing clear.
My instep arch not only keeps the ache,
It keeps the pressure of a ladder-round.
I feel the ladder sway as the boughs bend.
And I keep hearing from the cellar bin
The rumbling sound
Of load on load of apples coming in.
For I have had too much
Of apple-picking: I am overtired
Of the great harvest I myself desired.
There were ten thousand thousand fruit to touch,
Cherish in hand, lift down, and not let fall.
For all
That struck the earth,
No matter if not bruised or spiked with stubble,
Went surely to the cider-apple heap
As of no worth.
One can see what will trouble
This sleep of mine, whatever sleep it is.
Were he not gone,
The woodchuck could say whether it's like his
Long sleep, as I describe its coming on,
Or just some human sleep.

It's a poem of restlessness, the ambition kind, that spurs us toward greater achievement, only to find, sometimes, that there is nevertheless no satisfaction, no resting—

and restlessness then becomes a state of hauntedness, as we push over and over again toward a recognition of failure—our own—or what feels like failure, for why else are we not, after all that striving, finally at peace?

I say, "what feels like failure," because actual failure doesn't seem to be the case, here. Only a few apples remain unpicked, there seems only a single barrel that's not been filled, but these are depicted from, instead, the angle of failure—the speaker failed to get *every* apple, to fill *all* barrels. And of course, in the juxtaposition of the ladder and the mention of heaven in the first two lines, we are meant, I believe, to think of that other ladder, from Genesis, that appeared in Jacob's dream: that ladder led to heaven and actually reached it, albeit in dream. Here, in the Frost poem, we have a ladder far removed from Bible and dream; the real world comes short of those worlds, even as success does, apparently. The dream in the Frost poem is of an abundance that overwhelms but does not satisfy: "I am overtired / Of the great harvest I myself desired," presumably because of the unexpected responsibilities that the "great harvest" brings with it; how to keep up with "ten thousand thousand fruit," how impossible to avoid having some of them fall and be, consequently, deemed "As of no worth"? The speaker of the poem has learned too late, in his quest to have more, that having more means of course having more to lose. Is that a piece of knowledge that makes the getting there, in the end, worth it?

Would the committed artist say yes?

Is there, indeed, a choice?

The poem's ending has always troubled me because of its anthropomorphizing of the woodchuck, giving what had otherwise been a dignified poem a cartoonishness. But the subtle use of the word *just* in the final line rescues the ending. A comparison is set up between human and animal sleep; the latter is described as "long," as opposed to "just some human sleep"—one way to understand this is as a comparison between human, eight-hour, daily sleep and animal hibernation. But a more disturbing reading allows for the comparison to be not between durations of sleep but between qualities of sleep. The word *just* diminishes human sleep, pronounces it *inferior* to animal sleep. And indeed, the poem has suggested the problems with human sleep—we're beset with dreams that lead us to difficult self-awareness, lay bare the emptiness of our ambitions, point out that maybe we had it wrong from the start. This is presumably not the experience of a woodchuck, or any other animal that leads a life of pure instinct without the ability to reason, as we think of it anyway in human terms. Somewhere, in that word *just*, Frost suggests a reason for humans to envy

the woodchuck, even as Keats envies the nightingale—
which is to say, in vain. Again, we're human.

=

A quest to know, hand in hand with a boredom with
what is known already: is *that* it? I do believe that a certain boredom leads the artist to try new methods, take on
new subjects. Boredom can be a motivation for change,
and without change there can be no artistic growth.

But *is* it boredom, or is it restlessness as a form of
addiction to what the familiar can never give, namely,
the challenge of what's unknown, the self each time
differently surprised into what could be illumination,
could be corrosive despair—but the surprise—the surprise of it . . .

How is the restlessness that can lead to art all that
different from sexual restlessness? Aren't they *both*
sexual? Is this a truth in any broader sense, or just my
own truth? Do I betray myself?

=

A restlessness with the familiar, be the familiar thing
a body or a poem, an assumed agreement as to how
to conduct the body or a fixed number of ways agreed

upon for how to write a poem—it should rhyme, say, or it should make us feel good—a restlessness with the familiar doesn't *have to* lead to art, but it *can*. It can, as well, lead to danger. Risk is risk. But it's as if, for the artist, without risk there can be no salvation from a world that he or she finally cannot recognize as his or her own. Back to Adams, again, from *Beauty in Photography:*

> [The artist] commits himself to art precisely because he believes that he sees what others have not. If in the course of his training he discovers a master whose vision he wholly shares, then he becomes that person's advocate rather than an artist himself, and goes on perhaps to become a collector or teacher or professional critic. If however he finds that no one makes pictures like those he carries in his imagination, then he has to try to devise them. New pictures are the only way to avoid exile from himself. Should he fail, he is condemned to live by others' views, ones that must always seem inaccurate.

"To avoid exile from himself." The idea being that the artist must avoid an exile from the self, given that the artist is already, as if by default, in exile from the *rest* of the world, or from the majority of it. To be exiled from the self, as well, is to be lost indeed.

The problem, though, is that the self is never quite enough. We may select our own society, as Dickinson says of the soul, we may reside there for a time, especially—necessarily, I would say—during those times when we're making what we intend as art; but ultimately, we want, too, to be loved, and we want, by extension, what we make to be loved. That requires an audience outside the self. And in the tension between our understanding that what we make is finally only for ourselves to judge, and a nagging desire for confirmation from a world to which, deep down, we feel no real relationship or attachment—in that tension lies yet another restlessness, generative mostly of anxiety, a false sense now of triumph and now of defeat. It can destroy that other restlessness that made a way for the making of art.

 ☰

What is restlessness *for*?

Can't it be a condition of being human, and nothing else?

Must it *have* a purpose?

Does it?

 ☰

> Oh, what a thing is man! how far from power,
>   From settled peace and rest!
> He is some twenty sev'ral men at least
>   Each sev'ral hour.
>
> One while he counts of heav'n, as of his treasure:
>   But then a thought creeps in,
> And calls him coward, who for fear of sin
>   Will lose a pleasure.

Here, in the first two stanzas of his poem "Giddiness," George Herbert not only makes clear that human beings are by their very nature restless, but he also establishes a relationship between sin and pleasure. We would expect pleasure itself to *be* a sin, to be equivalent to it, and that is partly the implication here, subtly reinforced by the shared positions of the words *sin* and *pleasure* at the breaks for two consecutive lines. But as well, Herbert suggests that sin has a purpose, namely, to generate a fear that will make us avoid those pleasures that it would be a sin to enjoy.

And yet, as stanza one suggests, our restless nature is not apparently changeable, even given sin and the fear of it. Herbert spends another four stanzas giving examples of that restless nature, before explaining that the only remedy is to be remade on a daily basis by, as we'd expect from Herbert, God himself:

Lord, mend or rather make us: one creation
         Will not suffice our turn:
Except thou make us daily, we shall spurn
         Our own salvation.

In "Giddiness," Herbert laments our restlessness, hence the prayer for correction by God. When we put that next to the poem "The Foil," though, we learn that human beings are—at the core—more often than not unchanged by correction, seen here in the form of grief. Grief has been established by God as a means of highlighting sin—presumably, that we might by seeing it clearly understand more clearly the need to avoid it. And yet, and yet:

         If we could see below
The sphere of virtue, and each shining grace
         As plainly as that above doth show;
This were the better sky, the brighter place.

         God hath made stars the foil
To set off virtues; griefs to set off sinning:
         Yet in this wretched world we toil,
As if grief were not foul, nor virtue winning.

Our restlessness leads us inevitably to the sinning that we must then turn to God to be brought back from, notwithstanding that we slip inevitably again anyway, in spite of God. It is complicated—all the more so, when we remember that—according to Herbert—our restlessness is itself God-given, its purpose is to bring us eventually back to God, as a respite from the restlessness of ourselves. Here is "The Pulley":

> When God at first made man,
> Having a glass of blessings standing by;
> Let us (said he) pour on him all we can:
> Let the world's riches, which dispersèd lie,
>   Contract into a span.
>
> So strength first made a way;
> Then beauty flowed, then wisdom, honour, pleasure:
> When almost all was out, God made a stay,
> Perceiving that alone of all his treasure
>   Rest in the bottom lay.
>
> For if I should (said he)
> Bestow this jewel also on my creature,
> He would adore my gifts instead of me,
> And rest in Nature, not the God of Nature:
>   So both should losers be.
>
> Yet let him keep the rest,
> But keep them with repining restlessness:

> Let him be rich and weary, that at least,
> If goodness lead him not, yet weariness
>   May toss him to my breast.

Restlessness, then—for the Herbertian Christian, at least—can be generative, eventually, of salvation. Restlessness is divine and necessary, says Herbert; and without sin, the fear of it, and the temptation toward it, there would be no restlessness. By that logic, doesn't that mean it's at some level reasonable to sin, insofar as to do so is to be actively engaged in the machinery of eventual salvation?

=

Or is all of this mere rationalizing, an attempt to justify what we believe, somewhere inside, to be morally wrong? I'm thinking now of Shakespeare's Sonnet 110:

> Alas, 'tis true, I have gone here and there,
> And made myself a motley to the view,
> Gored mine own thoughts, sold cheap what is most
>   dear,
> Made old offences of affections new.
> Most true it is that I have looked on truth
> Askance and strangely; but by all above,
> These blenches gave my heart another youth,

And worse essays proved thee my best of love.
Now all is done, save what shall have no end;
Mine appetite I never more will grind
On newer proof, to try an older friend,
A god in love, to whom I am confined:
> Then give me welcome, next my heaven the best,
> Even to thy pure and most most loving breast.

How am I to know you're my "best of love," without "worse essays"—that is, without having tried others and found them inferior to you? Doesn't established friendship only find its established nature in the context of what is less so, is new? The idea, then, would seem to be that infidelity—sexual restlessness—is a necessary means of understanding the difference between mere sexual partners and the truly beloved. Is that true? It's true that value is meaningless without the concept of comparison. But where the body and, indeed, our feelings are concerned, the stakes escalate significantly.

Here is Thom Gunn's "My Sad Captains":

One by one they appear in
the darkness: a few friends, and
a few with historical
names. How late they start to shine!
but before they fade they stand
perfectly embodied, all

the past lapping them like a
cloak of chaos. They were men
who, I thought, lived only to
renew the wasteful force they
spent with each hot convulsion.
They remind me, distant now.

True, they are not at rest yet,
but now that they are indeed
apart, winnowed from failures,
they withdraw to an orbit
and turn with disinterested
hard energy, like the stars.

The restlessness Gunn describes here is a sexual one. The men are associated with a past that is likened to chaos, "each hot convulsion" suggests orgasm, the force behind it described as "wasteful," as in to no purpose, and their lives are described as being reducible only to the renewal of a force that's wasteful. Surely this is restlessness and it is sex. But it is a restlessness that—from the evidence the poem offers us, at least—generated nothing, just seems to have perpetuated itself and, even now, in the afterlife, the men aren't spared, not yet, anyway (leaving room, perhaps, for the hope of rest?). But they are "winnowed from failures," have energy, even if it is "disinterested" and "hard"—they are

not unbeautiful and not without their purpose, insofar as they are "like the stars": the stars are one way by
which we can orient ourselves, find our way home, or
take leave of it, for a life elsewhere. However sad they
may be, these men are the speaker's captains, like the
stars in their motion but also, implicitly, in their reli-
ability even as, incongruously, it is in their restlessness
that they are most reliable. Gunn gives to restlessness,
to sexual restlessness specifically, a strange dignity, almost, removing the men from the realm of moral judg-
ment, the speaker himself adding, as if casually, that
he only thought the men lived a certain way—he can't
be certain now, perhaps because the men are dead,
but it has always seemed to me that, in that phrase, "I
thought"—appearing at the poem's dead center, so that
the poem itself turns on possible doubt—that what
Gunn's speaker has come up against here is the slip-
periness of morality and the dangers of trying to give
any one shape or name or definition to morality.

Why should sexual restlessness be any less a part of
individual sensibility than the kind of restlessness that
makes some of us into artists?

=

There's a restlessness that keeps us up at night, the kind
whose catalyst isn't uncertainty, or a quest to know what

isn't known, but is guilt. Perhaps we can say it leads—
out of a desire not to feel the agony, the particular restlessness that guilt leads to—to a correction of behavior.
It doesn't erase mistake—mistake being a prerequisite
for guilt—but it can stop us from repeating the mistake, or what at least we believe to be, deep down, a
mistake. Right, or wrong—who can say?

—Oh but what is to become of me then, now that guilt's
gone away?

Beautiful Dreamer

I have thought of writing as a form of—or perhaps the record of—a resistance to difficult realities that we, as writers, nevertheless, as if unavoidably, make it our quest to look at all the more closely, even as we again resist them. I've also considered writing as both the result of and the enactment of a restlessness of imagination, a desire to abandon our selves to what we suspect we should resist, even as we know that to resist entirely would likely lead to a form of death-in-life, which is somehow worse than death itself—isn't it?

Years ago, I saw something that, by now, I believe I neither should nor shouldn't have seen: a young man leaned completely naked against a half-fallen tree in a forest clearing, while two older men variously had sex with him, doing the things men do with one another, but roughly, with the roughness especially of indifference coupled incongruously with desire—for desire is many things, but nothing like indifference. It was clear that all three of the players were there by agreement. Eventually, it was finished. The two older men left. The

young man, smiling, looked up and straight out toward
me. He'd known I was there, all along. He closed his
eyes, then. He slept. And I watched him sleep.

=

That's one version. And here is another:

Beautiful Dreamer

And when the punishment becomes, itself, a pleasure?
When there's no night that goes unpunished? The larger
veins show like map work, as in *Here winds a river,*
here a road in summer, the heat staggering up from it
the way always, at triumph's outermost, less chromatic
edges, some sorrow staggers. Parts where the mud,
though the rains are history now, refuses still to
heal over. Parts

                    untranslatable. Parts where, for whole
stretches, vegetation sort of strangling sort of makeshift
sheltering the forest floor. To the face, at the mouth
especially, that mix of skepticism, joy, and panic
     reminiscent
of slaves set free too suddenly. Too soon.—Which way's
the right way? New hunger by new hunger? Spitting
on weakness? Raising a fist to it? The falling mouth falls
farther. Opens. It says: *I was the Blue King. I led the*
     dance.

"Which way's the right way? New hunger by new hunger?" The catalyst for the poem was sexual, and in a sexual context these questions are especially troubling. "New hunger by new hunger" is one way of conducting a sexual life; whether or not it's the "right" way, whatever that might be, is debatable, but it's certainly true that to move from one sexual hunger to the next one can lead to trouble—though trouble is not automatically a *given*, just a possibility; to have emerged unscathed from risking that possibility is, for some, a very real part of sexual pleasure.

Poetry.

Sex.

There's a kind of sex that is less about power than about the unpredictability—and the flexibility—with which that power gets divided between and among the parties involved. Initially, in the scene I mentioned earlier, the young man had seemed the embodiment of weakness, the passive instrument of the two older men. But I eventually saw something like triumph in the young man's smile, and an absolute sense of control throughout his body, even as he allowed others to control it. It was as if he were instructing them exactly *how* and *when* to control it. The two older men, then, as weakness. And the young man as—what? pliant master?

How about: poet mastering, for now at least, his demons? That may seem a bit of a stretch, but it is also true that, though the poem arose from a sexual scenario,

I had somewhere in mind that the questions—"Which way's the right way? New hunger by new hunger?"—might be applied to writing: without the constant abandoning of one hunger for a new one, the desire to keep moving into discovery, how can a writer ever grow, either by deepening or by broadening his or her terms and terrain of inquiry? Any reluctance about this kind of motion, any preference for intellectual stasis, I'd determined to be weakness—easily worth spitting on, worth raising a fist to . . .

I say that I had these ideas in mind, but that's not quite accurate. For months after having written the poem, I in fact found it difficult to know with any certainty, if not the poem's meaning, then at least the meaning to which the poem might be gesturing. Many poets write toward a chosen subject, but I've always been the kind who writes from a supposedly clear space into a space of surprise, that is, where I find myself surprised—and not so pleasantly surprised, more often than not, surprised instead into a heightened awareness of something troubling. In "Beautiful Dreamer," punishment is so confusable with pleasure that it can become, like pleasure, addictive. Triumph is shadowed, ultimately, by sorrow. Freedom is a joy, but means also a removal of those constraints that, for better or worse, served as coordinates by which we at least knew where we were, not just geographically, but—given the tension between the concrete and the abstract world in this poem—morally, as well. In the context of morality, "Which way's the right way?" is a question that's always worth asking, lest we become too fixed, too prescriptive about right and wrong—history reminds us what *that* has led to. But it's also the case that to ask "Which way's the right way?" can imply not just that morality is flexible—as I believe it is, and should be—but also that a blurring of morality is possible, and in that blurring is the very real chance for us to *lose* our way. What then?

Well, one particular answer is that we can end up like the young man in the scene I witnessed. Sure, I've said he seemed the master of the situation, but master at what cost? If one holds, for now, the upper hand in negotiating sexual desire, is that power? *"I was the Blue King. I led the dance."* So? And?

Inevitably, every poem is in dialogue with other poems. When scrying my own poems for their possible intentions, I've often found it instructive to see what other poems are ghosting my own, and to think about why and how they are doing so. When I first began thinking about this essay, I knew I wanted to discuss in some way the relationship between experience, written response to that experience, and what might be meant by response *to,* versus expression *of,* any given experience. And I figured starting with one of my own poems would be reasonable, given how we can only rarely speak for the experiences behind the poems of others—we know what the poet chooses to *tell* us; in our own poems, we know the rest of it, what we chose to suppress. Not until settling upon "Beautiful Dreamer" as my starting-off point did I begin to realize how this poem gestures to at least two others. And, not coincidentally, both of them give a scenario in which a speaker in a desert scene comes upon something or someone who makes a statement or pronouncement, as the falling mouth does in my own poem, a poem written after I'd stumbled upon a scene in a woods—not a desert, but is it so far-fetched to think of this particular woods as a kind of moral desert, one at least where moral direction has become unclear?

"I was the Blue King. I led the dance." And here is Shelley's "Ozymandias":

> I met a traveler from an antique land
> Who said: Two vast and trunkless legs of stone
> Stand in the desert . . . Near them, on the sand,
> Half sunk, a shattered visage lies, whose frown,
> And wrinkled lip, and sneer of cold command,
> Tell that its sculptor well those passions read

Which yet survive, stamped on these lifeless things,
The hand that mocked them, and the heart that fed:
And on the pedestal these words appear:
"My name is Ozymandias, king of kings:
Look on my works, ye Mighty, and despair!"
Nothing beside remains. Round the decay
Of that colossal wreck, boundless and bare
The lone and level sands stretch far away.

The poem speaks, of course, to the ultimate hollowness of power, to its transient nature, and to how easily power and the arrogance that can attend it can be reduced to tokens that themselves shatter, decay, become wreckage. It's a poem I haven't read or thought about in many years, and yet the resonances between it and my own poem seem unmistakable. *"I was the Blue King. I led the Dance."* It sounds like power, but it is said in the immediate wake of a confusion of skepticism, joy, and panic, of slavery and a terrifying freedom, and of a series of questions to which the mouth gives as answer only a statement about a power that is a thing of the past. As if the past were a beautiful dream from which it would be better never, never to wake—is *that* it?

But then there is this poem, untitled, the third in Stephen Crane's book-length sequence *The Black Riders and Other Lines*:

In the desert
I saw a creature, naked, bestial,
Who, squatting upon the ground,
Held his heart in his hands,
And ate of it.
I said: "Is it good, friend?"
"It is bitter—bitter," he answered;
"But I like it
Because it is bitter,
And because it is my heart."

What the creature says in those last three lines may not seem at first a statement about power. If anything, they arise from the condition I describe in "Beautiful Dreamer," where punishment—if we can agree that to eat one's own heart is a form of punishment, the kind we'd expect to find in the Greco-Roman Hades or in Dante's Hell—has become pleasure. But I find also in the creature's statement something about the power that can come from knowing exactly where one stands—he has no illusions about the taste, for example: it is bitter, and the certainty of that bitterness—why else say three times that it's bitter?—is both a form of power and, as if consequently, a source of pleasure.

Another certainty: the creature knows the heart is his own. Would it be worse, then, if he were eating someone else's heart? That's what is implied, though the reasons aren't stated. Maybe it has to do with how we can never really know another's heart, so it's better to eat of what we know; even if we can't know our own heart entirely, we know it better than we know another's. There's also the fact that others can never know our hearts as well as we ourselves do; that is, the pleasure here is not just that he is eating a heart that he knows, but also that the eater of the heart is not a stranger. And again, these certainties translate into a kind of power.

If both the Shelley poem and Crane's poem lie somewhere behind my own—and I believe they do, though my conversation with them was not at all a conscious one—then does that make my own speaker's statement both a statement about the delusions of power and at the same time about how certainty—which is a form of clarity, delusion's opposite—is itself a power that's very real? Yes, I think. Both. And somehow neither. Power is many things—perhaps conundrum, especially.

$=$

We write from experience—whether an event actually happened to us, or we experienced it secondhand: hearsay, a news story, something we witnessed of another's experience. And every experience we have, for all its being in the immediate present, is in the context of the world as we've come to know it, which is to say in the context of history—our own, and the longer-ago history that is the backdrop *for* our own. Similarly, the context of literary history is the backdrop for our own contributions to literature. The poems by Shelley and Crane both concern, quite differently, the abstraction of power. Each comes to a conclusion, but this is different from a resolution of the problem, as it were. Abstraction—from justice to death, from death to love, from love to mercy—will always resist resolution. At best, we can arrive at a stance with *respect* to a given abstraction; this can feel like resolution, though it is only respite—which is better than nothing, however.

The irresolvability of an abstraction like power, combined with the very real, human impulse to give to shapelessness a form, is the catalyst for the particular field of inquiry that we call art—in this case, poetry— and the inquiry is an ongoing one, across history, because the "problem" being investigated resists solution, and yet we as humans can't resist trying to find solution. The poem is at once the evidence of having made the attempt, and the enactment of that attempt. It is also, however unconsciously, our contribution to the long tradition of those who have made the same attempt and the same failure to resolve the irresolvable. We write in response to being human, and to those before us who have done the same; it's in this sense that I can see "Beautiful Dreamer" as being in dialogue with Shelley and Crane.

But there are other dialogues. We are, each of us, uniquely haunted. I spoke earlier of demons—the countless manifestations of transgression toward which—and by which—we are variously driven. In addition to these, there's everything we remember, for better *and* worse, everything we've loved or not loved, everything we've lost that nevertheless refuses, somehow, to go away. I believe we write as a means not of laying these ghosts and demons to rest, but of giving them, however briefly, a context within which we feel we've brought under control what we know full well we *cannot* control. The poem is a form of negotiation with what haunts us—or to put it another way, is the interior dialogue we have with our other selves, insofar as what haunts us is, in part, who we are.

=

Two poems have, of late, been haunting me. One is this untitled one that I'll call "Paul," by Lorine Niedecker:

> Paul
> when the leaves
> fall

from their stems
    that lie thick
        on the walk

in the light
    of the full note
        the moon

playing
    to leaves
        when they leave

the little
    thin things
        Paul

The other poem is one by W. S. Merwin, called "Rain Light":

All day the stars watch from long ago
my mother said I am going now
when you are alone you will be all right
whether or not you know you will know
look at the old house in the dawn rain
all the flowers are forms of water
the sun reminds them through a white cloud
touches the patchwork spread on the hill

the washed colors of the afterlife
that lived there long before you were born
see how they wake without a question
even though the whole world is burning

Each of these concerns loss, and does so in the context of the ongoingness of the natural world. The trees in Niedecker's poem may have been reduced, now the leaves have fallen, to "little / thin things," but we know their foliage will be restored, unlike Paul, who may be the poem's addressee, but could as reasonably be a personal loss that comes to mind, for any number of reasons, in the fall. Likewise, the mother in Merwin's poem is dying; she assures the speaker that he won't be alone, but for company she offers not herself but the natural world, not an afterlife but the colors of it, an afterlife that is vegetal, floral, and as indifferent to human affairs as to the apparent fact that "the whole world is burning." And yet, despite the subject matter, there's a beauty to these poems that has to do, in part at least, with artistry. In the Niedecker, how rhyme appears in each stanza, but each time just a little differently; the sheer spareness of her imagery. The somewhat surreal gorgeousness of imagery in the Merwin, though his poem has its own kind of spareness, in addition to a particular spareness that it shares with Niedecker's poem, in being both short and unpunctuated. Is it that loss has a beauty to it? Or do we try to make loss easier, by making it beautiful? Wouldn't we miss, maybe more than a little bit, what it felt like, to have lost, to have been lost? Never to have known sorrow—for all its awfulness, without it, what would the texture of a life be?

=

> Failing to fetch me at first keep encouraged,
> Missing me one place search another,
> I stop somewhere waiting for you.

So ends Walt Whitman's "Song of Myself," breezily and absolutely establishing an intimacy between himself and the "you" of his reader. Nearly a hundred years later, Muriel Rukeyser opens her poem, "Effort at Speech between Two People" with these lines:

> : Speak to me.   Take my hand.   What are you now?
>   I will tell you all.   I will conceal nothing.

And here is the stanza with which the poem ends:

> : What are you now?   If we could touch one another,
>   if these our separate entities could come to grips,
>   clenched like a Chinese puzzle . . . yesterday
>   I stood in a crowded street that was live with people,

> and no one spoke a word, and the morning shone.
> Everyone silent, moving . . . Take my hand.   Speak
>   to me.

One way of thinking of a poem is, in fact, as an effort at speech between two people. To "touch one another," have "our separate entities . . . come to grips"—to solve, or at least to try to solve, the particular puzzle of human estrangement.

Is that really, though, what a poet wants, an erasure of estrangement, speech between two people? Or is the effort—the word I keep leaning on in Rukeyser's title—is the effort enough? Inadvertently, I think, we speak from our own hauntedness to the hauntedness in others, those readers with whom our private poem, as if magically, resonates—that stranger who, having read the poem, says: "I have been there, known that place, though I did not know it entirely, or not at least like this. And I have felt the same." But again, this resonance—which is a form of response—is at best the hoped-for but not exactly expected result of a dialogue that's inadvertent; it's not the reason for writing, or it isn't for me, at least. I think I write not to understand struggle and to somehow by understanding it come to some sort of peace with it, but to understand just enough to know how much more there is, still, to be understood; not an end, then, to struggling, but a stepping more deeply into it.

I spoke earlier of the interior dialogue that the writer conducts with the ghosts, the demons that are his or her other selves. Lately, it feels less like dialogue than a matter of having looked upon those other selves clearly, then looked away, and then looked steadily, slowly back—as if for what? confirmation? There is a difference between risk and a leap of faith. Maybe writing is both. The risk is a self-knowledge that can at best be dispiriting, at worst destructive. And the leap of faith? That it will all, eventually, have been worth it? To whom? And how?

The decision—if it is one—to look at the self, the world, and one's place in it squarely, to step out of the mythology that we daily present to the world as our actual selves, is not an easy one, but for the writer it's crucial. This is what Rukeyser is getting at in "The Poem as Mask," in which she repudiates having taken on the persona—which is the Latin for "mask"—of the singer Orpheus:

When I wrote of the women in their dances and
    wildness, it was a mask,
on their mountain, gold-hunting, singing, in orgy,
it was a mask; when I wrote of the god,
fragmented, exiled from himself, his life, the love
    gone down with song,

it was myself, split open, unable to speak, in exile
     from myself.

There is no mountain, there is no god, there is memory
of my torn life, myself split open in sleep, the rescued
     child
beside me among the doctors, and a word
of rescue from the great eyes.

No more masks! No more mythologies!

Now, for the first time, the god lifts his hand,
the fragments join in me with their own music.

"No more masks! No more mythologies!" And yet, the poem is always at some level a mask—we choose as poets what to include, what not to, from the experience that we write from, the experience of being who we are, which is ever-shifting and multifarious. The poem serves as mask behind which we find the courage to allow the fragments—our various selves—to "join in [us] with their own music." Courage, because as the fragments unite, they can coalesce into a meaning that we might prefer to have left shattered.

Who is the dreamer?

What makes him beautiful?

What was the dream?
Or not a dream—   What happened?

=̄

John Ashbery ends his poem "Street Musicians" with these lines:

> Our question of a place of origin hangs
> Like smoke: how we picnicked in pine forests,
> In coves with the water always seeping up, and left
> Our trash, sperm and excrement everywhere, smeared
> On the landscape, to make of us what we could.

We make of the fragments of self a form that holds, briefly—that's the poem—then we watch it shatter again—which is, I suppose, that space that the poem fooled us into believing we'd left behind us, for a time, world of fragmented selves, hard truths, glinting ambiguities to be negotiated, navigated through as we make our disoriented way forward, or what we have to believe is forward. Like being mapless in tough territory, and knowing, somewhere inside, we'd choose this life, and this one only, if in fact we could choose.

Poetry, Love, and Mercy

I've been thinking lately that the lyric poem is always at some level a testimony at once to a love for the world we must lose and to the fact of loss itself—and how in that tension between love and loss that the poem both enacts and makes a space for, there's a particular resonance that I'll call mercy, wherein we experience, incongruously, a bittersweet form of joy in what at the same time remains disturbing: not mortality itself, but our uniquely human consciousness of mortality, and of abstractions like love and loss. Mercy, then, not in the Judeo-Christian sense of a means toward and/or an opportunity for salvation, but as a kind of respite—not oblivion, but a strangely heightened consciousness of the stakes of mortality. The effect for the reader—for this reader, at least—is to be as if bodily shaken: I'm made to see the world more intensely, my love for it deepens, even as my sorrow does—without which, I wouldn't know what love is, to begin with.

Here is Laura Jensen's "The Red Dog":

You know that he is going to die
as soon as I tell you
he is standing beside me
his hair in spikes and dripping
from his body. He turns his head.
Canadian geese
all of them floating along the shore.
The red dog is swimming for them
only his head shows now
they flap into a curve and move
farther along the bay.
You know that he is going to die
this is the time for it
this is the best time for it
while there is a way to vanish
while the geese are moving off
to be their hard sounds
as their bodies leave the water.

The poem begins in death and in groundedness—the eventual death of the dog, who is earthbound, "standing beside" the speaker, who is also earthbound—as is, presumably, the addressee. But the poem closes on vitality, both physical and audible, the "hard sounds" of geese in flight. Already, then, we might say there's a pitching of death against life, the two of them in balance, in tension—both, I'd say.

Another way to look at it is in terms of trajectory: the poem's trajectory, what I like to call the psychological trajectory of a poem, is from death to life. This is hardly consistent with the usual notion of mortality's trajectory, which is from birth/life toward eventual death. But it *is* consistent with the trajectory of what those who believe in it call the afterlife, resurrection, reincarnation. And there is some notion of an afterlife that seems to get implied in the poem's last three lines, a transformation that attends the departure from water to air, which is to say, coincides with ascent, as the geese become something less general than geese, more specifically the "hard sounds" that we associate with geese in that moment of their leaving the water.

We might also say that the poem's trajectory represents half of the full circle of the natural world: while humans, and dogs, come to life, then die, the natural world continues, seasonally, the trees coming into leaf, losing their leaves, and flourishing again, come spring. At some level, we exist once against a backdrop of on-goingness. The dog is what we all are—a living thing in the context of death. But he can't know this; *we* do, or as the speaker says, "You know that he is going to die." And our knowing this is what allows for life and death—love and loss—as, for humans, inextricably intertwined, each giving to the other a poignancy, a resonance. This is the gift of the poem to us, the readers.

"The red dog is swimming for them / only his head shows now / they flap into a curve and move / farther along the bay." That is the three-dimensional picture of an action and its actors. Nothing we can't easily have seen before. But the context that the poem gives to the scene charges both action and actors with an added dimension that isn't visual but—all at once, somehow— is emotional, existential, psychological. The dog, the geese—they are what they are, and more than that. For a moment, we see as poets do, we see the world beneath "mere" world, or perhaps as accurate, the world that limns "mere" world. There is a cost to this, of course—who wants to be bedeviled with thoughts of mortality all the time? But at the same time, our recognition of what is to be lost, and our dismay at that, is a way of understanding value and love: we wouldn't balk at losing what meant nothing to us—which is to say, it meant something. Which is to further say: we remember; we loved.

=

A friend calls, he tells me he's heading out to trim the bittersweet and raspberries along the marsh behind his house. Look at his hands: how old they are, I can see them now, the rugged tenderness with which they negotiate the delicate new growth of leaves, tendrils. The hands reddening easily in the cold of the air. The salt of it. Already I'm not certain that *mercy* is the right term for what I mean, at all.

=

Where, for example, is the mercy in Muriel Rukeyser's poem "The Minotaur"?

Trapped, blinded, led; and in the end betrayed
Daily by new betrayals as he stays
Deep in his labyrinth, shaking and going mad,
Betrayed. Betrayed. Raving, the beaten head
Heavy with madness, he stands, half-dead and proud.
No one again will ever see his pride.
No one will find him by walking to him straight
But must be led circuitously about,
Calling to him and close and, losing the subtle thread,
Lose him again; while he waits, brutalized
By loneliness. Later, afraid
Of his own suffering. At last, savage and made
Ravenous, ready to prey upon the race
If it so much as learn the clews of blood
Into his pride his fear his glistening heart.
Now is the patient deserted in his fright
And love carrying salvage round the world
Lost in a crooked city; roundabout,

> By the sea, the precipice, all the fantastic ways
> Betrayal weaves its trap; loneliness knows the thread,
> And the heart is lost, lost, trapped, blinded and led,
> Deserted at the middle of the maze.

The poem's subject is that Minotaur, half man, half bull, who was the bodily incarnation of the curse put upon Pasiphaë, queen of Crete, who was made by the gods to feel lust for and then conceive with a bull. The queen's husband then imprisons the beast in a labyrinth—those are the bare essentials, anyway, of the story. Rukeyser's poem focuses squarely on the Minotaur's psychological state, that state in particular of having been betrayed (his only crime, after all, is to have been born) and from there how betrayal is an affront to one's pride, an affront that is catalyst for madness and for a loneliness that affords a space for fear—in this case, a fear of suffering itself. The poem becomes itself a labyrinth— psychological, emotional—analogous to the physical one that contains the Minotaur.

Another labyrinth occurs sonically here, on at least two levels. First, there's that of rhyme, of which there are but three in this poem of twenty-two lines— three rhymes that do and don't announce themselves. The most frequent rhyme is with the word that ends line 1, *betrayed*. It only rhymes *exactly* with *afraid* (11) and *made* (12), but makes what is called a consonan-

THE ART OF DARING   79

tal rhyme with *mad* (3), *head* (4), *proud* (5), *pride* (6), *thread* (9), *blood* (14), *world* (17), *thread* again (20), and, again, *led* (21). Consonantal rhyme is, as you can see, one where two words rhyme by virtue of their being anchored by a vowel and the same consonant. A second consonantal rhyme occurs, then, between *straight* (7), *about* (8), *heart* (15), *fright* (16), and *round-about* (18). Finally, there's the exact rhyme between *stays* (2), *race* (13), *ways* (19), and *maze* (22).

The poem is a rhymed poem, which is to say there is a sonic pattern, but the pattern is irregular, as unpredictable as a labyrinth. At the level of rhyme, we find our way, lose it, pick up the thread again. Note, too, how this sense of return is reinforced by how the poem opens with "trapped, blinded, led," the same phrase that occurs in the penultimate line of the poem—it's an odd reinforcement, because what it emphasizes is a return to what, presumably, we would hope to escape, a sense of disorientation; there's a neatness to having the poem begin and virtually end with the same phrase. It feels like closure, the satisfaction of an answer, and yet if the answer means the inescapability of imprisonment, what then?

I mentioned two sonic labyrinths. The second occurs metrically. Without going into elaborate detail about prosody, I'll point out that the poem is constructed of three kinds of lines: hexameter, pentameter, and a single tetrameter line at line 11. Of the pentameter lines, lines that have five stresses, line 6 is a good example:

No one again will ever see his pride.

Of these pentameter lines, some come in at ten syllables, some at eleven, and one (line 19) at thirteen. So, there's again regularity and an irregularity, within the pentameter lines themselves. Within the poem overall, we might say there are pentameter lines, yes, there are hexameter lines (lines with six stresses—lines 1, 3, 9, 12, 20, 21), but they work as the rhymes do: they appear without predictable pattern, though the lines themselves are a *form* of pattern. The effect, at the levels both of rhyme and of meter, is that we hear a pattern and get adjusted to it, only to be thrown by a shift in pattern. Pattern tends to put us at ease, psychologically—it gives us something to lean on, as it were. But the pattern here is of disruption. If Rukeyser's poem feels good in the mouth, in the ear—and I believe it does—that pleasure is not unlike what's at least part of the pleasure of being in an actual maze, namely, a slight fear, at the possibility of getting lost, that possibility getting pitched simultaneously against our sense that there is, in fact, a pattern, a system—we have only to understand it, and we'll find our way out—or so we assure ourselves, trusting perhaps too much in pattern and its ability to hold up in the face of chaos, the unexpected, things as unpredictable as betrayal, Rukeyser's subject here.

Is it that a poem makes something pleasurable of what shouldn't be? Is that one of its methods of persuasion? There is a pleasure to rhyme and to meter at an almost atavistic level: again, pattern is at the heart of it, and we respond to pattern early in childhood, with nursery rhymes, songs, and so on. These patterns—and, I would say, the interruption of them at unpredictable moments—are the pleasures of Rukeyser's poem, and they do in fact persuade *me* as a reader; I find myself eager to figure out the patterns, intrigued by the artistry, excited to learn what's behind the sense of release at the poem's end, a sense that has everything to do with how the last line, one of the poem's only strictly iambic pentameter lines, is preceded by two hexameter lines that differ slightly from each other—there's a cumbersome sound to them, in comparison to the easy fluidity of the final line—listen:

Betrayal weaves its trap; loneliness knows the thread,
And the heart is lost, lost, trapped, blinded and led,
Deserted at the middle of the maze.

And yet, this is a poem in which there *is* no escape—that last line may *feel* like release, sonically, but what it *says* is that the Minotaur—well, by now, it is less specifically the Minotaur, and more generally the heart—the heart remains both trapped and deserted, less in a physical labyrinth than in the more abstract maze of betrayal. Rukeyser's poem meditates on, without resolving, what it means to have been betrayed, hardly what we might choose to think about for long. But the patterning of the poem seduces, and allows us to look more closely upon betrayal with some degree of pleasure, as if pleasure were a balm to make this particular reality more bearable. Is *that* mercy? Some briefly sustaining form of pleasure, as we confront the predicament of our vulnerable selves?

=

Both of the poems I've looked at, so far, bring together in their different ways pleasure and a difficult reality. I don't know that this has to be the case, in order for the mercy effect to take place, whereby we come to see the world in its deeper complexity and, as a consequence, something inside us stirs at the thought of it, the world we must lose, the fact of loss—I don't know if pleasure and some sorrow have to be in place, but they usually seem to be. And usually the pleasure part happens at the level of pattern of one kind or another. Here's a poem that seems entirely peaceful, though very little ostensibly happens. The poem, by the seventh-century BC Archaic Greek poet Alkman, survives as a fragment, though it has a contained quality to it, the translation is Guy Davenport's:

> The valleys are asleep and the mountaintops,
> The sea cliffs and the mountain streams,
> Serpents and lizards born from the black earth,
> The forest animals and beeswarms in their hives,
> The fish in the salt deep of the violet sea.
> And the long-winged birds.

What happens in this poem? Everything is sleeping. That's not exactly an event worth writing a poem about, we might say. Or as might be said in workshop, the poem risks being overly static, at least in terms of its narrative pattern. Davenport has—wisely, I think—chosen here to forgo Alkman's metrical patterns in favor of a fairly literal and ultimately more accurate translation. But what's retained is Alkman's structuring. Alkman begins with geography—earth, mountains, water (the streams, and the sea that the cliffs must border)—then he moves to the biological life associated with that geography: reptilian, mammalian (the forest animals), apian, and aquatic. The poem has for its first five lines been a single sentence composed as a list. Then, as if it were an afterthought, the more abbreviated "And the long-winged birds," inhabitants of the air, the one zone that had been omitted earlier. The birds are the only element assigned an adjective that connotes action: "salt deep," "violet sea," "forest animals," the adjectives in those instances describe, respectively, taste, color, place—all of them static, while "long-winged" gives us the means by which the birds physically navigate through the air. The effect is that the poem shifts from seeming static—all is asleep—to active; the birds, too, are sleeping, but in their being described in terms of their means of passing actively across the sky, activity enters the poem. This, coupled with how the organization, the careful guiding of our eye from landscape to the life that adds its own activity *to* that landscape, is what makes the poem feel complete. The fact that all is asleep—is inactive— resonates with what we know but are not told: that, eventually, all will wake again into the activity we get some hint of in "the long-winged birds."

It takes awhile to realize that what's missing here are human beings—even the bees seem undomesticated; I don't see human-made hives here. And it's in this omission of humankind that the poem takes on a further resonance. Is something being said about the relative insignificance of human life and, more significantly, of human ambition when it comes to the natural world? Is the poem itself what stands in for a human presence, evidence of an impulse to make art, what distinguishes us from the animals? Does the poem take place in a time before human civilization, and is civilization meant to seem then as inimical to those moments of peace that the poem assigns to the natural world? These are only a few of the questions that are generated in that space just past where the poem itself ends. And these questions are where we begin to think existentially and metaphysically about ourselves, what we hadn't expected, the poem itself giving no suggestion that we would have to leave the safer world, we might say, of lovely description, for the always potentially more troubling world of introspection. Pattern swayed us, seduced us—pattern, and beauty in the form of restraint, simplicity.

Centuries later, in his poem "Oceans," Juan Ramón Jiménez will describe in a different context what happens in Alkman's poem, the way in which stasis can be deceptive, it can distract us initially from realizing how much has in fact changed:

> I have a feeling that my boat
> has struck, down there in the depths,
> against a great thing.
>   And nothing
> happens! Nothing . . . Silence . . . Waves . . .
>
> —Nothing happens? Or has everything happened,
> and are we standing now, quietly, in the new life?

(translated by Robert Bly)

At a dinner party, my friend the novelist is insisting that forgiveness is real, that it doesn't mean a hurt is forgotten, but somewhere inside we remain both mindful of it and able to give it a context that allows us to move meaningfully forward with the one who has done us harm. To my mind—and I say as much to my guests—forgiveness has no meaning, or no relevance finally, since it can't exist without an absolute forgetting of hurt; and once we've forgotten it, what is left to forgive?

It's at this point that another guest—a former nun, a fact that seems somehow to matter—tells us of a recent neighborhood incident, in which one dog killed another dog. "What's weird," Kathe says, "is that one of the dogs was named Justice, the other one's name was Mercy—I forget whether Mercy killed Justice, or the other way round."

"Yes, but the difference it makes is crucial," shouts yet another guest, Maverick, pounding the table, an energetic discussion ensuing before I remind my guests of what I myself have almost forgotten: we are speaking of dogs.

$=$

So much of poetry seems rooted in this tug-of-war between seeing a thing for what it is and our human impulse to see a thing for what it resembles. Often enough,

the costs of that impulse, as well as its limits, become
the poem's subject beneath the more overt subject. Here
is Brigit Pegeen Kelly's "The Dragon":

> The bees came out of the junipers, two small swarms
> The size of melons; and golden, too, like melons,
> They hung next to each other, at the height of a deer's
> breast,
> Above the wet black compost. And because
> The light was very bright it was hard to see them,
> and harder still to see what hung between them.
> A snake hung between them. The bees held up a snake,
> Lifting each side of his narrow neck, just below
> The pointed head, and in this way, very slowly
> They carried the snake through the garden,
> The snake's long body hanging down, its tail dragging
> The ground, as if the creature were a criminal
> Being escorted to execution or a child king
> To the throne. I kept thinking the snake
> Might be a hose, held by two ghostly hands,
> But the snake was a snake, his body green as the grass
> His tail divided, his skin oiled, the way the male member
> Is oiled by the female's juices, the greenness overbright,
> The bees gold, the winged serpent moving silently
> Through the air. There was something deadly in it,
> Or already dead. Something beyond the report
> Of beauty. I laid my face against my arm, and there

It stayed for the length of time it takes two swarms
Of bees to carry a snake through a wide garden,
Past a sleeping swan, past the dead roses nailed
To the wall, past the small pond. And when
I looked up the bees and the snake were gone,
But the garden smelled of broken fruit, and across
The grass a shadow lay for which there was no source,
A narrow plinth dividing the garden, and the air
Was like the air after a fire, or the air before a storm,
Ungodly still, but full of dark shapes turning.

The speaker watches the scene, looks away, looks back again; no bees; just a shadow that can't be accounted for on the garden. That's the overt narrative. But the poem is very much, also, about seeing, about the determination to see exactly, correctly, and in doing so to make the unknown knowable: as is also true with naming, if we know a thing, we possess it, we make it our own. This desire to see is immediately apparent in Kelly's poem, as the speaker shuttles from bees to the specificity of the swarms' size—given to us in terms of the visible, "the size of melons"—and to the swarms' color; we learn not only that "they hung next to each other," but also that they did so at a particular height—again, not in terms of feet or inches, but of something more exactly visible, "at the height of a deer's breast."

It's at line 12 that the tug-of-war I mentioned earlier emerges, that moment when the snake's passage is compared to three very different things: "as if the creature were a criminal / Being escorted to execution or a child king / To the throne"; or, thinks the speaker, "the snake / Might be a hose, held by two ghostly hands." And, as if recognizing her having yielded too entirely to an impulse to see in a way that ultimately shields us from seeing accurately, the speaker reminds herself: "But the snake was a snake . . ." The conundrum of figuration is that it can be a way of seeing more clearly what hasn't been seen before—a snake being carried by swarms of bees—and yet it can distract us from accuracy—not a criminal or child or hose, but a snake. I would add, as well, that figuration's ability to distract has its own two-sided nature: it can equally distract us *away from* and straight *into* disturbing realities. Until line 12, Kelly's poem exists firmly in the natural world, rather like Alkman's poem, devoid of the human and of the difficulties that attend what we call civilization. But at the mention of the criminal and the child king, the concepts of justice and of the wielding of power emerge, both of which interpose by implication a moral system whose ambiguities are worlds removed from the simplicity of natural instinct. This is true, as well, for the hose—a garden hose, I'm presuming. In a poem that takes place in a garden—especially a poem that will end with a biblical vision, complete with the smell of broken fruit—it seems reasonable to think of Eden, where we are told transgression led to the need for agriculture, in which hoses of course figure.

From hoses to "the way the male member / Is oiled by the female's juices." Easily the strangest moment in the poem. And again, it is a moment when the speaker moves from the literal ("his skin oiled") to the figurative and immediately back to the literal ("the greenness overbright"). It's as if that figurative moment were an interruption, an intrusion: without it, we'd see the snake clearly enough—his skin oiled, the greenness overbright—but with it, we get the sexual and, by extension, the idea of reproduction and fertility—an instance, I'd say, of figuration distracting us away from reality; for, as the speaker will soon acknowledge, the snake isn't exactly an example of vitality—"There was something deadly in it, / Or already dead."

If Kelly's poem concerns vision, it also concerns the limits of vision and of knowing. I think this is why the poem ends with the otherworldly, the appearance of a shadow that cannot be accounted for. But the poem is also very much about our resistance to the inexplicable, our human confidence in reason. The poem's ending enacts this confidence by returning again to figuration: "the air / Was like the air after a fire, or the air before a storm, / Ungodly still, but full of dark shapes turning." Which explains the air, but the shadow continues to elude all reason, remains as "Something beyond the report / Of beauty," which is to say, something to which the poem can bear witness, but cannot explain.

Love, mercy—how do they figure, here? I think our desire to see is a manifestation of love. As I mentioned earlier, to see is a form of possession, and presumably we only want to possess what we've assigned value to; we care about it more than we care about something or someone else. What we don't love—what we don't desire—we try to shut our eyes to. The merciful part of figuration allows us not to shut our eyes, but to briefly see what's difficult as something less so. We escape, as it were, through imagination. But figuration can also make us mindful again of difficulties we'd almost forgotten. Where's the mercy in that?

Love and Mercy. Mercy and Justice. Like stepping-stones across a stream. I forget the name of the stream. Something about how blue his eyes were, opening, yes, how like steel his eyes were.

"I wanted to be sure to reach you; / though my ship was on the way it got caught / in some moorings." So go the opening lines of Frank O'Hara's "To the Harbormaster," which uses the metaphor of a ship at sea as a way of speaking about human failure, the ways in which we don't always live up to our best intentions. I've become increasingly interested in how poems work in relationship to a life as it becomes—to stay with O'Hara's imagery—unmoored, whether voluntarily or not, how poems in turn become, if not islands of sanctuary, then unexpected harbors at which to, if only temporarily, drop anchor. Maybe this is another form of mercy that a poem affords us.

As for love—

There is mere existence. And there's experience. Pitched further—more resonant—than either of these, a poem, whether we're reading one or writing one, more actively grapples with, refines, and embodies experience, the experience of choosing—rather than to pass through the world—to instead take into ourselves the world with all of its sometime brutalities, and sometime joys. This taking in of the world is a kind of loving. A sustenance. Never mind that it will not save us. Every poem is, somewhere, both a form and an act of love.

Penetration

Which One's the World?

When I was a child, one of my favorite books—still a favorite, actually—was Randall Jarrell's book for children *The Bat-Poet*, with illustrations by Maurice Sendak. Partly, the book is about a bat who wants to be a poet. Because of this, he doesn't exactly fit in with the other bats, and this idea of not belonging, of desiring communion in a world that one is forever outside of—simply because of being who one can't help being—is very much Jarrell's subject. It's also about the longing for an audience, which the bat eventually finds in a poetry-appreciating chipmunk. And as we watch the bat encounter an owl, then write about that encounter, observe a mockingbird and then put what he's seen into words, we find that the book is also about the ability of poetry to capture experience in a way that allows us to return to that experience once it's over.

I was five when that book came out, and of course I just loved the book for its immediate story, for the animal drawings, for how the bat eventually finds out that he can be who he is, and find something like a home in the world. Sometime in my thirties, I finally read the adult poetry of Randall Jarrell, and when I did, I was shocked to see—in his collection *The Lost World*—three of the four poems from *The Bat-Poet*. How could children's rhymes have a place in an adult book of poems?

It's an instance where context makes every difference. *The Lost World* opens with one of Jarrell's most famous poems, "Next Day," told by a woman who, in middle age, while shopping for groceries, suddenly understands that she's past her prime, that she looked for happiness in the wrong places, and that

> As I look at my life,
> I am afraid
> Only that it will change, as I am changing:
>
> I am afraid, this morning, of my face.

The poem ends by opening out to an understanding, more broadly, of the human condition itself:

> But really no one is exceptional,
> No one has anything, I'm anybody,
> I stand beside my grave
> Confused with my life, that is commonplace and
>   solitary.

The poem that immediately follows this poem is "The Mockingbird," which had appeared in *The Bat-Poet*, though without a title. It's straightforward enough: a description of the mockingbird's habits (as observed by our bat-poet), as he goes around "imitating life." We see him waxing territorial, driving all the other birds from the yard, even a cat, stealing everyone else's songs. Finally, at day's end, the poem also ends:

> A mockingbird can sound like anything.
> He imitates the world he drove away
> So well that for a minute, in the moonlight,
> Which one's the mockingbird? which one's the world?

That confusion between the world and the imitation of it—to a child, to this particular child—spoke to the magic of a bird who could copy sounds so exactly. But reading those lines in the wake of the lines with which "Next Day" concludes, I understand something very different from magic, something more about how frightening it can be to no longer know for sure what reality is or has ever been. Is this my life? Was the life I remember having lived ever really like that? Did I really have certain ambitions, and have I truly ended up somewhere very different? Or, as I once put it in one of my own poems, "Would-Be Everlasting":

> How much
> was true? Not native to it, how much has from that
> country been my own rough translation?

So much of Jarrell's poetry concerns a desire to return to childhood, to the specific image of a mother holding her child in her arms. Such a desire returns us to a time when to want or need anything was to have it provided, a time before we became shaped by the complications that make us adult human beings. Jarrell believes—correctly—that we never really lose something of the innocence of childhood, or at least of the memory of it, and a consequent longing for it. We still, as adults, want to be held, and to be able to trust unthinkingly, in spite of what we know of the world.

The final poem—again, untitled—that the bat composes, before succumbing to hibernation, appears in *The Lost World* as "Bats." It's about the vulnerability of a bat at birth, and the mother's instinct to feed and protect her young. As the poem closes, the mother returns, with the baby bat clinging to her, to the rafters where all the other bats live:

Their sharp ears, their sharp teeth, their quick sharp
   faces
Are dull and slow and mild.
All the bright day, as the mother sleeps,
She folds her wings about her sleeping child.

As a child, of course, I saw this scene simply for what it is: comforting, safe, a way of thinking about mothers that resonated with my own experience. *The Bat-Poet* ends shortly after this poem, with the bat returning to the company of the other bats, who have already begun hibernating: "he yawned, and screwed his face up, and snuggled closer to the others." The End. The instinct to re-create that embrace of the mother here gets expressed in more general communing.

Again, it's intriguing to see the poem appear in an adult collection. In the context of *The Lost World,* "Bats" becomes a poem about the inner child. It speaks to the world of fairy tale that characterized childhood and somehow continues to haunt us. A few poems after "Bats," Jarrell offers us "The House in the Wood," which revisits fairy tale, what he calls "the story // We make of life." In the poem, an adult speaker returns to a sort of fractured Hansel and Gretel scene—it's hard to say if it's a dream, or a way of looking at the subconscious:

If I walk into the wood

As far as I can walk, I come to my own door,
The door of the House in the Wood. It opens silently:

On the bed is something covered, something humped
Asleep there, awake there—but what?

Where are we, exactly? "We are far under the surface of the night," and "It is only a nightmare. No one wakes up, nothing happens," Jarrell says, before concluding his poem:

> Here at the bottom of the world, what was before the
>   world
> And will be after, holds me to its black
>
> Breasts and rocks me: the oven is cold, the cage is
>   empty,
> In the House in the Wood, the witch and her child sleep.

It's the same scene with which "Bats" ended, the mother replaced by a witch, but a witch who has abandoned her desire to cage children and cook them, in favor of the maternal gesture of sleeping protectively with the child. This is the lost world. "A bat is born / Naked and blind and pale"—those are the opening two lines of "Bats." When I read those lines in the context of *The Lost World*, I understand Jarrell to mean more than that. He seems to speak to our metaphysical blindness and nakedness, the vulnerability that never quite leaves us, despite adulthood. More disturbingly, that vulnerability only increases, the further we get from anything like a protecting adult figure. We're left, as adults, to protect ourselves and, with luck, each other.

The Lost World came out one year after *The Bat-Poet*. For Jarrell, childhood gets left behind, and it never leaves us. He seems to have understood that there's something poignantly adult about childhood, and that we adults are not so far from the children who believed in magic—talking chipmunks, poetry-reciting bats; indeed, our belief in that world can continue to sustain us, even as it soberingly reminds us of all that we've lost.

Heaven and Earth

It began as mere fascination. I read the poems of Sappho as a college freshman, and noted immediately how often her expressions of sexual desire intersected with heart-felt prayer to the goddess Aphrodite—prayers sometimes for the satisfaction of longing, sometimes for release from it. At the time, this was as revelatory as it was shocking for me, the sheer idea that sex and prayer might exist within the same space. Wasn't this what they meant by blasphemy? If so, why did each line seem charged with what I can only call a holiness?

From Sappho to Greek tragedy where, over and over, the entire plot revolves around the conflict between human desire and divine law or will. In Euripides's *Hippolytus,* for example, Theseus's wife Phaedra is made by the gods—Aphrodite, specifically—to feel sexual desire for her stepson Hippolytus. Hippolytus, as it turns out, is not only not attracted to her, but to no women whatsoever, and especially has no time for worshipping goddesses like Aphrodite, for which reason the goddess punishes him—a punishment that begins with Phaedra's infatuation with him. (Is Hippolytus gay? It's never stated, of course—it wasn't a concept that meant anything in the way that it does now; also, I wouldn't have known to call it gay back then—I hadn't yet come to understand why I dated no women, and could make no sense of what seems obvious to me now, my crush on my roommate Scott.) Driven to despair at not having her sexual feelings requited, Phaedra hangs herself, leaving a note suggesting she's been raped by her stepson. Theseus finds the note, curses his son, and the gods make good on the curse, smashing him and his team of horses upon some rocks by the sea.

What is the moral here? That Hippolytus should have overcome his instincts, and not only slept with a woman, but with his stepmother, no less? That the stepmother should have overcome/suppressed her desires?—but how, if they were divinely willed? That the gods are cruel, because they inflict sexual longing upon us? Is that longing, then, a bad thing—a form of punishment?

So Oedipus learns that he has fathered two daughters by his own mother. So the Minotaur—perhaps the ultimate outsider, half bull, half man—is the result of the gods driving the queen of Crete to want to have sex with a bull; and it is art, in the form of Daedalus, that master craftsman, that turns her wish—her desire—into reality. And so it is that King Creon, resisting the lawlessness that the new god Dionysus encourages, is made by Dionysus to dress in drag in order to secretly witness the religious rites the women of Thebes are performing in honor of Dionysus. And in the religious fervor of those rites, Creon's mother literally tears his head off, only to be brought back to reality, to the recognition of what she's done, by Dionysus. End of play.

I called the Minotaur an outsider before, but another way to see him is as the most truthful representation of human beings—one half reason, the other half an instinct that is animal. Calibrating the two halves, so that neither part entirely overcomes the other, is the particular work of being a human being. To deny the existence of either half is not reconciliation but denial, which, however motivated by fear, is ultimately failure. But that denial is as old as the ancient Greeks. After all, the Minotaur was considered a monster, and was imprisoned in a labyrinth, conveniently out of sight.

Why should it be monstrous, that we have animal desires, including sexual ones?

The gods themselves have a lot of sex, in Greek mythology. Zeus, the king of the gods, is constantly raping young women, simply because he wants to. Leda is among the more famous ones, raped by Zeus in the form of a swan. Without that rape, we'd have no Helen of Troy, no Trojan War, therefore, so no Aeneas fleeing Troy, which will lead ultimately to the Roman Empire, from which will come Western Christian tradition as we know it. Does that make Leda's rape acceptable, then? Even holy, given the divinity of her assailant? Is it sacrilege to call it holy, or to say it's not?

For the Greeks, sex and divinity, if not exactly compatible, find an uneasy but somehow necessary co-existence within the larger realm known as Fate. Zeus explains in Homer's *Iliad* that he himself doesn't have ultimate control of the Trojan War's outcome—he administers Fate, he doesn't determine it. Fate seems the equivalent of God/the Word at the start of Genesis—that element before which there was nothing, and against which all resistance is a waste of time. To my way of thinking, this removes all blame from our human lapses. And yet, without blame—which is to say, without a sense of right and wrong—we erase morality itself: what then? What I spoke of earlier, that reconciling of our reason and of our more basic animal instincts, is precisely what morality is, and it is ongoing and ever shifting. For all the damage that's been done in the name of morality, we'd be lost without it, as we'd be lost without sex, and without a belief in things for which there's no tangible proof—which doesn't have to be divinity. Atheists, after all, do believe in other abstractions—just not the particular abstractions of God, Heaven, Hell . . .

Morality gets a bad name because it's so often equated with inflexibility. From Hester Prynne's having to wear a scarlet letter on her dress as an announcement of her adultery, to the ongoing rash of gay teenage suicides, we can see what this kind of morality has led to. The purpose, I think, of morality should not be to define human behavior, but to temper it. Not to tell us it's wrong to be gay, but to show us that homosexuality is one of many forms of sexual identity that, to become whole human beings, we need to learn to incorporate into and calibrate with all the other parts of identity—race, tastes in music, our capacity to love, for example, our fear of the vulnerability that love comes with . . .

I've known men for whom a history of childhood sexual abuse has made sex undetachable from violence and fear. They either resist the sexual as something suspect, or they throw themselves as if self-destructively into it, temporarily quieting the part that won't shut up inside. One of these men has suggested to me that almost worse than abuse was the unwillingness to believe it, on the part of the adults whom he told, or tried to tell—an unwillingness, I think, to acknowledge the fact and force of the sexual in our daily lives. When I think back to health class and sex education when I was a kid, I have no recollection of being told it was abnormal or wrong to be gay. No, something worse happened. The existence of homosexuality wasn't even addressed. A form of brainwashing, it seems to me now, however inadvertent. It's a situation that was paralleled by the Sears catalogs I thumbed through as a child, and the shows I watched on television, where no black face ever appeared; if society says you don't exist, or implies you shouldn't, how long before, deep down, you almost come to believe it?

You could say that all of this has to do with society, not religious belief systems. But our society as we've come to know it here in America was created by religious zealots—the Puritans, as well as French and Spanish Catholics. Despite a separation of church and state, religion has remained all but equivalent to law, for many—most?—Americans; the rest of us have become, at best, highly suspicious of anything that smacks even vaguely of the spiritual. To choose either side means missing something—something of that complicatedness that gives depth to a life, texture. Human beings aren't purely rational, or irrational either. Herbert White, the eponymous serial killer in Frank Bidart's poem, recognizes, with a certain horror, what he's done—he has, that is, what we might call a soul or, at the very least, a sense of moral accountability. Meanwhile, the most persuasive religious writers—George Herbert, for example, John Donne, Gerard Manley Hopkins, the Augustine of *Confessions* (though less and less, after that)—are persuasive precisely because they acknowledge the fact of desire, its seductiveness, our own desire to be at times seduced by it. It's almost as if the impulse to resolve a conflict that's irresolvable is the generative engine for the work itself—or, in Herbert

White's case, the conflict and the need to resolve it generate, for better and worse, a life in full, lit by an honesty that we at last can't hide from. We look in the mirror; the Minotaur stands before us—this time, we don't look away.

Heaven and Earth

For days now, vertigo. Conqueror birds. Place where
suffering and a gift for it for a moment meet,
then go their separate ways. *I keep meaning to stop,*
to wait for you. Places where, all but untrackably, fear—
which is animal, and wild, and almost always
worth trusting—becomes cowardice: fear given
consciousness of a finite existence in the realm
of time—what exists,

      and doesn't. Last night,
a stillness like that of moss; like permission when it's
not been given, yet not withheld exactly. Across the
 dark—
through it—the occasional handful of notes: someone
else out there, singing? or myself singing,
and the echoing after? I didn't know,

        or want to. A map
unfolding, getting folded back up again, seeming
sometimes—even as I held it—to be on fire:
It had seemed my life. What am I, that I should stand

so apart from my own happiness? The stars did
what they do, mostly: looked unbudging, transfixed,
like cattle asleep in a black pasture, all the restlessness
torn out of them, away, done with. I turn beneath them.

What am I, that I should stand so apart from my own happiness?

Why should it be monstrous, that we have animal desires, including sexual ones?

Why yearn for an existence where all restlessness has been torn away, is done with?

Why not think of restlessness as a star that we turn beneath?

I think—no, I know I began writing as a way to explain myself to myself—no, as a way of trying to maybe unblame myself for what I couldn't help being: not just a man attracted to other men, but a man of almost constant restlessness, on one hand; and on the other, a man for whom fidelity—sexual fidelity in particular— holds genuine value, despite everything, by which I mean my belief in the need for risk, my belief that monogamy is a straitjacket rooted in a religious impulse to suppress instinctive desire, my fear of that stillness- like-a-living-death that I see in so many couples who pride themselves on having been together forever, with- out straying.

When I first came out, I was told the best thing about being gay is that there are no rules; we decide for ourselves what we mean by family, relationships, devotion. The problem, though, is the usual one that freedom comes with. I could do anything; what shall I do then, or not do? And if there's no one who will tell me yes, or no, how do I know if I've done the right thing, if there's no way left of telling what's right or wrong, except for what we believe for ourselves, inside, which brings us back to faith, doesn't it?

The zebra grass outside my studio has shot into amber, October flower. To watch the flowers, swaying in this wind that hasn't stopped since last night's storm, is a form of prayer—or for me it is. Even as sex is, or can be, as I long ago said, and still believe. If I pray, it's in these ways. I don't know why the grasses in the wind strike me as beautiful, or why that beauty seems a form of divinity. I don't know why the body—penetrating, penetrated—can seem luminous, a kind of sacrament, why a group of men having sex beneath a dock on a summer night crammed with stars becomes its own communion. The poet, as Keats famously said, possesses negative capability, an ability to be in the presence of troubling questions without giving in to the need to resolve them, without—ideally—feeling that need at all.

Why am I who I am? the mind wonders—or perhaps the soul does. It's the body, though, without which we couldn't know this world, couldn't touch it, see it. And the body, instead of *Who am I?* says *Here I am: Do with me what you will.*

Daring

Foliage

Eighteen years with a man I'd once credited with having saved me from losing myself—a man who still, despite increasing estrangement, comes the closest to what I'd call a soul mate. Then almost six years with a man whose sexual prowess and respect for mine—and to be fair, his kindness—for a long time held at bay my growing impatience with—what, his stability? His predictability? Is that why I left him for a nine-month roller coaster of a relationship with a charismatic, binge-drinking alcoholic whose recklessness I sometimes confused with the heroic, but sometimes saw—correctly—as the mask for a vulnerability that kept winning me over, until at last it didn't?

"And in the end, the love you take is equal to the love you make," the Beatles once sang. Maybe that's true. All I know is that, at fifty-four, I find myself single for the first time in my adult life. The dog looks up at me. I look up to the lithograph that hangs above my fireplace. I bought it at an auction, was drawn immediately to how it had been listed in the catalog—no title, just "Allegorical Etching." Allegory for what? It's from around the 1930s, I think, and it depicts what appear to be the three Graces turning away in a combination of sorrow, shame, and fear. They seem to have been dismissed by the two figures who glare disdainfully at the Graces from the picture's left: an imperial woman, arms crossed, whose skirt, hooped and Elizabethan, is made entirely of peacock feathers; and at her feet, a satanic-looking harlequin, hooked nose, cap-and-bells that more resemble horns. The two seem victorious, as if after a battle of moral wills. They seem decidedly immoral, or to be flouting all assumed conventions about morality. Next to the lackluster Graces, they're practically radiant with their cool indifference to expectation, and with their refusal to treat instinct—and perhaps an instinct for the wilder pleasures, in particular—as a horse to be broken and stabled. I think it's this that I instantly recognized when I saw the piece at auction; and it's why I positioned it front and center in my living room, as a kind of visual embodiment of what I've made my rallying cry—and, as it's turned out, a career, in the process.

=

There's a kind of shadowland that one body makes,
    entering
another; and there's a shadowland the body contains
    always

within itself, without resolution—as mystery a little
   more
often, perhaps, should be . . . For a moment, somewhere
between the two, I can see myself as I begin to think
you must see me: a stranger to helplessness,
spouting things like *To know is to live flayed* and
   Ambition
means turning the flesh repeatedly back—toward the
   whip,
not away, I can still hear myself saying that, believing
   it—
now it all sounds wrong . . .

I'm still committed to the idea that restlessness sets risk into motion, and that the two are catalysts for imagination and, by extension, the making of art. But this afternoon, I wonder: if it's all led to the writing of poems, a bewildering twelve books of them (bewildering, given how it seems I write hardly ever), hasn't it also led me through a string of increasingly reckless, unstable, even dangerous engagements when it comes to my life *off* the page? Which is to say that, after over twenty years of writing in favor of a life of risk, of asserting that there can no more be art than there can be a fully lived life if it doesn't involve routinely daring to act in the face of risk—after all of that, at last I question the costs of it. What's a poem worth risking, when it comes to a life?

Or when does art become the means of rationalizing otherwise questionable behavior? Certainly it didn't begin that way. Rather, a crisis in life led me to write the first poems I was willing to call my own. I've said it had to do with being married—to a woman—and slowly coming to understand myself as a gay man. But guilt was more to the point—guilt over betraying someone's trust in me by having sex with others. And for whatever reason, the pressure of that got played out on paper (as opposed to a canvas, or a cello, or a therapist's couch). It seemed instinctive to write a way through—and the result was the small controversy of my first book. I say controversy, because I was described as a writer of daring, who took the risk of speaking about the usually unspoken in a kind of language that itself took risks. What's useful for me to consider now—to remember—is that I had no intention of being daring. Is it daring, then, if we're simply doing, acting, speaking as we would anyway? I had no idea I was writing what might shock, even offend a reader. Is it risk, if we don't know that it is?

My memory of how the Cumaean Sibyl receives prophecy in Virgil's *Aeneid* is that Apollo rides her as if she

were a horse, digging his spurs in. But because the language seems sexually charged, I've always thought that
she's also getting fucked by the god. And in the course of
getting simultaneously ridden, goaded, and fucked, she
opens her mouth and prophecy spills forth—nothing
she herself is aware of, she just does the talking.

"As if I believed utterly," as I once put it in one of my
own poems,

> what
> legend says about violation—how it leads
> to prophecy, the god enters the body, the mouth
> cracks open, and a mad fluttering, which
> is the future, fills the cave, which is
> desire, *luck and hazard, hazard and luck* . . .

I don't believe in taking risks in order to write, and yet
a risk-taking sensibility—if it is a risk to plumb questions that most people avoid trying to answer—has had
everything to do with what I write about and how I
write about it. It's one thing, though, to think in such a
way that a poem results, quite another to engage in behavior off the page and have a poem be the result. I like
to think the distinction is intention. To have ended up
in a dicey situation is different from having sought one

out, especially in the name of making poems. I've never exactly fallen into that latter category—poetry is, after all, the transformation of experience, not the transcription of it—but I know full well that many of my poems are composed of the more resonant experiential left-overs of actual incidents, not the incidents themselves, but what flashes off of them, stirring memory, provoking questions, until what's left, it seems but the being

                              alone with
    what, rather than trying to escape the mind's grasp,
    refused to leave it, instead kept changing its shape
    inside it: now risk,

                    now faintheartedness, now
    a kind of youth again, now pleasure as the effacement
    entirely of what, inside us, we couldn't bear
    looking long at, no,

                    not a moment longer . . .

    =

Whether we dare to do a thing, or dare someone else to do a thing, it would seem that daring is only daring in the context of risk—humiliation, pain, maybe even a life. It's daring for an adult to dare a child to jump off a roof; the risk is arrest, for injuring a child. But it isn't daring for the child to jump, if she has no awareness

of mortality, of the fact that she could be seriously
harmed. Daring has everything to do with a sometimes
crippling knowledge, the thing that children lack, which
accounts for their fearlessness—which isn't bravery,
at all. I think this in part is what Robert Duncan is getting at, in "Childhood's Retreat":

It's in the perilous boughs of the tree
out of blue sky   the wind
sings loudest surrounding me.

And solitude,   a wild solitude
's reveald,   fearfully,   high   I'd climb
into the shaking uncertainties,

part out of longing, part   daring my self,
part to see that
widening of the world,   part

to find my own, my secret
hiding sense and place, where from afar
all voices and scenes come back

— the barking of a dog,   autumnal burnings,
far calls,   close calls—   the boy I was
calls out to me
here the man where I am   "Look!

I've been where you
most fear to be."

The child dares himself, insofar as he's aware he could fall, but the adult has the fear that comes with knowing what the fall could lead to. The same things are at stake, but the adult understands it more fully. Is this not like the making of art? In a sense, then, the child dares the man, who becomes briefly a child again, and he takes a chance. He climbs higher. The poems of mine that I consider successful are the ones where some part of me seems to have dared another part to do something that, if I were fully aware of it, I'd never do: use a certain word, let a sentence find its own wilderness, speak on subjects I'd more likely suppress talking about in my daily life. One risk, I suppose, is of losing the control that has always been part of my sensibility; another, that I won't be understood, or I'll somehow be judged. But the risk of not daring is that I'll fail to have been entirely myself—the risk of not daring, you might say, is artifice, inauthenticity.

$=$

Love, too, of course, involves risk. But there would seem no daring to it, since who thinks of the risks?—

possible heartbreak, inevitable loss (to which love necessarily commits us), and worse. And yet who doesn't want it?

In one version, I'm hitting him—hard, repeatedly; in another, he's kicked the back screen door in, threatening to beat me into the ground. We got here how?

＝

The deeper one gets into what eventually amounts to a career, the harder it becomes to incorporate daring and risk into it. As in life, if we're lucky, we grow more comfortable, successful, and accordingly more aware that there's more to lose. So there's a resistance to changing what's in place already. Meanwhile, we're aware also of there being daily less time left, which can bring fear. This issue of time, it seems to me, should spur us on to live even more adventurously—if not now, then when?—but mostly it doesn't, or so it seems when I look around me. Why risk what it's taken us all our lives to at last get hold of? Or if we haven't gotten it by now, why try, why bother? And yet for the artist I think an appetite for a certain recklessness is crucial, if the work is to not only extend itself, but also deepen, and meaningfully complicate itself.

> Often it is hard to know when the middle game
> is over and the end game beginning, the pure part
> that is made more of craft than it is of magic.

So says Jack Gilbert, in "Me and Capablanca." The best magic, in poetry, will always involve craft, of course, but unself-consciously, on the poet's part—instinctively, rather. But I take Gilbert's point, his implied one, that there's a difference between craft and magic. Magic, I believe, is the result of daring, of knowing the risks, albeit not consciously—and acting anyway. It's the part we never expected, while we were thinking somewhere more closely about image, line, diction. But even magic can become predictable, which explains the later careers of many excellent poets—there's too often a magic that they've shown us for years, though there's no doubting it's still magic. The challenge is in getting the magic to manifest itself differently and to the surprise, most importantly, of the artist himself, the kind of thing that seems to be at work, for example, in Louise Glück's taking on of the long line and a language that risks being prose, but instead reinvents lyric, in *A Village Life*. Or consider Frank Bidart's all but abandoning the long persona poem he's so known for, in favor of a shorter, compressed poem that seems more haunted because it is detached from persona. Or how Henri Cole has shifted from his earlier, more baroquely detailed work to a poem whose sparseness throws the poignancy of human struggle into greater relief.

Can we call these writers daring? Hard to say, without knowing the degree to which their changes have been conscious or instinctive. But the results are poems whose voices remain recognizable while surprising us with how they've grown and continue to do so. It is terrifying to walk away from what one has mastered. To me, it feels like daring.

≡

Damascus

Split by the light, wrought golden, one of a thousand
    cars stunned sun-blind,
crawling westward, I remembered a day I stopped for
    an old snapper,
as huge as, when embracing ghosts, you round your
    arms.
Who did I think I was to lift him like a pond,
or ballast from the slosh of hull swamp, tarred as he
    was, undaunted,
that thrashed and hissed at the worst place to try to
    cross,
where the road plunged east, the lumber trucks

swept daily down from the blue hills
past winter-ravaged toys blanching by makeshift
    crosses.
An old sea shimmered in the asphalt.
Spared over the mirage to ancient footpaths, he lunged
    again,
and spit, turning his oddly touching head toward the
    project
of the steep embankment. Such were the times.
Hardwired, the way. Cross here or die. Die crossing.

In this poem by Deborah Digges, it's the snapping turtle that's hardwired. It has chosen its path by instinct, not by any desire to risk crossing a major highway, indeed without knowledge of any risk. It's the speaker who's daring: "Who did I think I was to lift him . . ." She's aware of the risks: he could bite her, for one—he's thrashing and hissing—and she herself has to cross the dangerous highway with this wild cargo in hand. Meanwhile, at the sentence "Such were the times," something shifts. The turtle no longer seems the reference or context. The times, for a turtle, presumably don't change all that much. "Such were the times" seems more attachable to the speaker, or perhaps to her generation—as if to say, that's how it was for us, back then: "Cross here or die. Die crossing." As if it were a credo of sorts, a way of life to be committed to. A recklessness. Or willfulness. A form of daring. I read this in the context of art-making, in part because Digges was a poet, but also because of the poem "Fence of Sticks," which follows "Damascus" (and serves as end to her book *Trapeze*), a poem that addresses, among other things, the history of making art—of the makers, specifically, and the relevance, if any, of that history to the contemporary artist. It's difficult as well, though, not to read the end of "Damascus" in the context of the poet's death, an apparent suicide. And in the context of daring, to wonder—is suicide a form of it?

For a time, I thought so. To know what's at stake, and to be willing to risk losing it, seemed about as daring as daring gets. But my mistake was in thinking risk really figured. I've since come to associate suicide more with despair—a literal absence of hope, or a belief in that absence, so there being nothing to live for; where's the risk, in that case?

Maybe daring is akin to an abandoning of the self to something not entirely knowable. In that regard, it's a bit like faith. Suicide is something else. Not abandonment. As a friend of mine put it recently, "True suicide is commitment"—a counterweight, presumably, to the loss of control that suicide also seems to equal.

In the earlier mentioned "Fence of Sticks," Digges asks, "Weren't there times worse than this for art?" She speaks

of "those who, rather, bristled were they *understood,*"
"those who'd rather hang themselves than call truth
heresy," "[t]hose for whom art was not an occupation,"
"[t]hose who refused to make it easy," "[t]hose who died
having said too much."

I had to pull myself away to write is this not happiness?

That's how the poem ends.

＝

Is it risk, for
example, if what gets lost goes unregretted? Or if there
is any risk, then where, except awhile in the head?

So I asked, once, in *Speak Low,* where I also spoke of "humiliation's / not-so-strange allure." Where I wondered:

That part about the body
asking for it,

to be broken into—is that the first, or last part?

First came the mind fuck, for which I was ready, I guess,
for hadn't I gone there, a complete stranger's place, to
get to which I had to pass through neighborhoods each

of whose seediness got routinely trumped by that of the next one? I stripped on arrival, as I'd been told I would. He asked if I understood what I'd agreed to: to trust him, to do exactly what he said, to resist nothing. And I understood. I said I did.

In his bedroom I could see more clearly how much bigger he was—more muscular than me, but also maybe a good hundred pounds heavier. So, though I wasn't restrained ("Today," he told me, "the ropes are here, in your head"), I felt at once overpowered, should I need to save myself—though from what, if I trusted him? I was thrilled, afraid, shaking, and I somewhere trusted him.

But when he tried to fuck me, I resisted, and he became enraged. ("Resistance on a submissive's part, particularly if the dominant doesn't know them well, can be very difficult to interpret," I've since read in Jay Wiseman's *SM 101: A Realistic Introduction.*) He told me he was definitely going to fuck me now, but without a condom on; and having said that, he made me beg him to breed me, meaning fuck me bareback, and I begged him to. He fucked me slowly, deliberately, without a condom, then rough, to make it hurt on purpose. He made me say I loved it. He made me love it, I want to say, but that can't be true. He withdrew, jammed his cock in my mouth, came inside it. And when I cried, he told me to fucking grow up. He knocked me to the floor and kicked my head and chest with the boots I only now noticed, mesmerized, he'd never removed.

This is not an episode from childhood. This was just last year.

=

A friend and I have been texting about promiscuity, specifically about his decision to give it up completely, or pretty much completely. I asked him why.

It got lonely.
And too easy.

                              I get that. And you're
                              not lonely now?

No. Not like that.
That's a different
type of loneliness.

                              I see the difference.

Do you?

I used to think promiscuity was one of the more resonant manifestations of transgression, and insofar as I equated being gay with transgression, promiscuity amounted almost to a kind of membership card, a badge of honor, even, and certainly the space within which to observe and engage in the various configurations of power that can both give rise to and destroy relationships, whether with the beloved or with a stranger—to either of which there's an intimacy attached, or can be.

To put intimacy at risk, to put the body at risk—is this daring? The more I observed men get multiply, randomly, routinely barebacked by total strangers, the more I began to equate promiscuity with virtual suicide. Or with the despair, the nothing-left-to-lose, that I'd associated with suicide. And, as with suicide (commitment as a form of power that counterbalances a sense of powerlessness), I think promiscuity has a great deal to do with power—the feeling of conquest and/or of being conquered. But for all that, more and more I think promiscuity's not daring at all, and not transgression—not when everyone can seem to be engaged in it, as indeed they seem to be, in the sauna, in the steam room, in the back room where the slings can be found. Or put it this way: the potential risk of promiscuity is to become cliché—the kiss of death for poetry; indeed, for all art.

Divine Wrath

(Adélia Prado, translated by Ellen Doré Watson)

Three days after I was wounded
—who knows whether
by God, the Devil, or myself—
it was seeing the sparrows again
and the little clumps of clover
that told me I hadn't died.
When I was young, those sparrows
and lush leaves alone were enough
for me to sing praises,
dedicate operas to the Lord.
But a dog who's been beaten
is slow to go back to happy barking
and fussing over his owner
—and that's an animal, not a person
like me who can ask:
Why do you beat me?
Which is why, despite the sparrows and the clover,
a subtle shadow still hovers over my spirit.
Whoever hurt me, forgive me.

"Whoever hurt me, forgive me."

What does that mean?

=

Increasingly, daring, when it comes to a poem, has come to mean restraint, at least for me. It's not lost on me that restraint also figures into the BDSM community and the leather scene more generally. There, restraint and submission don't have to equal the relinquishing of control, and the same goes, I believe, for poetry. Power is fluid, ideally, which is perhaps to revise a bit: maybe daring more involves the calibration of release and restraint, the risk being that things can go too far in either direction.

One of the most daring poems ever is Jean Garrigue's "The Grand Canyon." Four sentences long, of which here are the opening three:

Where is the restaurant cat?
I am lonely under the fluorescent light
as a cook waddles in her smoky region visible through
    an open arch
and someone is pounding, pounding
whatever it is that is being pounded
and a waitress cracks with the cowboys lined up at
    the counter
lumberjacked, weathered and bony

intimates, I would guess, of the Canyon,
like the raven that flies, scouring above it,
of the hooked face and the almost flat sleek wings.

Where is my cat?

A single-line sentence. The second coming in at nine lines. The third at half a line. The material here is conversational, demotic. Intimate, to some extent, though in that shift from "Where is the restaurant cat?" to "Where is my cat?" the cat that belonged more generally to the restaurant is now attached to the speaker alone, or that is how the speaker has come to think of the cat, which suggests something of how alone she feels, as if the cat were all she could lay claim to, despite being surrounded by people, or perhaps because of that. The other thing that turns out to have made the speaker feel alone, existentially so, is the Grand Canyon itself, which Garrigue proceeds to describe in the poem's fourth and final sentence, one hundred eight and a half lines long, a sprawling sentence that, among many other things, both enacts and pitches the vastness of history up against the smallness of self. It takes daring to write a sentence that long and complex. It takes daring, too, though, to write a sentence like "Where is my cat?" And sheer nerve, to put the two next to each other.

Here's the end of Randall Jarrell's "90 North":

Here at the actual pole of my existence,
Where all that I have done is meaningless,
Where I die or live by accident alone—

Where, living or dying, I am still alone;
Here where North, the night, the berg of death
Crowd me out of the ignorant darkness,
I see at last that all the knowledge

I wrung from the darkness—that the darkness flung
    me—
Is worthless as ignorance: nothing comes from nothing,
The darkness from the darkness. Pain comes from the
    darkness
And we call it wisdom. It is pain.

A nine-and-a-half-line sentence, followed by a one-and-a-half-line sentence strung across two lines. Then "It is pain," the sentence that I've often thought might have been the hardest—the most daring—to write. To write it means stepping free of the syntactic and grammatical complexities of the sentences before, free of the mirroring ("nothing comes from nothing, / The darkness from the darkness"), it means leaving that safety where embedded clauses allow the mind to stall, to resist conclusion, for the colder air that so often attends clarity—here, that clarity is both syntactical and psychological, and feels decidedly hard won, even painful.

Release, restraint. Lengthy, complex sentences; short and simple ones. Dominant, submissive. Power steadily shifting back and forth between them. When did syntax and life become indistinguishable from one another? And if the balancing of release and restraint is a form of daring in poetry, what about in life? How wide, exactly, is that space between what I'm willing to try to do, and what I reasonably can?

The Darker Powers

Even if you're right,
and there's in fact a difference
between trouble unlooked-for, and
the kind of trouble we pursued,
ruthlessly, until at last
it was ours,

                what will the difference
have been, finally? What I've
called the world continues
to pass for one, the room spins

same as ever, the bodies
inside it do, flightless, but
no less addicted to mastering—
to the dream of mastering—the very
boughs through which
they keep falling without
motion, almost,
that slowly, it seems they'll fall
forever, my
                    pretty consorts, to whom
sometimes—out of pity,
not mercy, for
nothing tender
about it—I show the darker
powers I've hardly shown
to anyone: *Feel the weight of them,*
I say, before putting them back,
just behind my heart, where they blacken
and thrive.

≡

All summer, I resisted writing this essay. Something inside me refused. Only when I considered that the essay
itself might be a form of daring (what's an essay, after
all, but, by derivation, an attempt, a venture, from the
Latin for "to test"—to risk failure, therefore)—only then

was I able to sit down, put pen to paper, and pretty much in one sitting write it out the way some part of me must already have thought to arrange it, for it all came swiftly, though not without struggle. And real fear. The risk of seeming confessional. What needs to be told, versus what should be. The coming to grips with mistakes that, however much I've learned from them, have brought along with learning a fair amount of hurt, and sorrow.

To have spoken here of what I've hardly shown to anyone, then to put it all back—just behind my heart, where it blackens and thrives— And now what?

꞊

Respect or shame, it's pretty much your own choice, is how it once got explained to me. Who can say if that's right? But whatever else this is, it's the life I've come to. I'd dare it again. Tossing poem of a life spent at sea— restless, for sure, but no, not sorry. Or not mostly. If I've been restless, then as a compass can be, and still be true.

Acknowledgments

"Little Gods of Making," "On Restlessness," and "Beautiful Dreamer" were originally delivered (March 25, 27, and April 1, respectively) as the 2008 humanities lectures at Washington University in Saint Louis. The lectures were sponsored by the Interdisciplinary Project in the Humanities in Arts and Sciences and the Assembly Series.

"On Restlessness" appeared in *New England Review* 30/1.

"Poetry, Love, and Mercy" was delivered May 2, 2008, as the Judith Lee Stronach Memorial Lecture on the Teaching of Poetry at University of California, Berkeley. The talk was later published in a limited edition by the Bancroft Library, University of California, Berkeley, 2009.

"Which One's the World?" appeared on *Reader's Almanac,* the official blog of the Library of America, December 13, 2011.

"Foliage" appeared in the *Kenyon Review,* Fall 2014. The passage about the Cumaean Sibyl is excerpted from a brief credo (also entitled "Foliage") that appeared in the *Kenyon Review.* The discussion of Garrigue's "The Grand Canyon" borrows from my discussion of that poem online at *At Length,* in volume 4 of the "Short Takes on Long Poems" series. My poem "The Darker Powers" first appeared in the *Massachusetts Review* LIV/1.

Permissions Acknowledgments

CARL PHILLIPS is the author of twelve books of poetry, including *Silverchest, Double Shadow,* and *Quiver of Arrows: Selected Poems 1986–2006.* He is also the author of *Coin of the Realm: Essays on the Life and Art of Poetry,* and the translator of *Philoctetes* by Sophocles. His awards include the Los Angeles Times Book Prize, the Kingsley Tufts Poetry Award, and the Kenyon Review Award for Literary Achievement. Phillips teaches at Washington University in Saint Louis.

The text of *The Art of Daring: Risk, Restlessness, Imagination* is set in Warnock Pro, a typeface designed by Robert Slimbach for Adobe Systems in 2000. Book design by Wendy Holdman. Composition by BookMobile Design and Digital Publisher Services, Minneapolis, Minnesota. Manufactured by Bookmobile on acid-free 100 percent postconsumer wastepaper.